BEHOLD

Behold!
She is coming with the clouds
and every eye will see Her.

Lauren Sleeman

CHIRON PUBLICATIONS • ASHEVILLE, NORTH CAROLINA

© 2021 by Chiron Publications. All rights reserved. No part of this publication may be reproduced, stored in a retrieval system, or transmitted, in any form by any means, electronic, mechanical, photocopying, recording, or otherwise, without the prior written permission of the publisher, Chiron Publications, P.O. Box 19690, Asheville, N.C. 28815-1690.

www.ChironPublications.com

Interior and cover design by Danijela Mijailovic
Printed primarily in the United States of America.

ISBN 978-1-63051-972-8 paperback
ISBN 978-1-63051-973-5 hardcover
ISBN 978-1-63051-974-2 electronic
ISBN 978-1-63051-975-9 limited edition paperback

Library of Congress Cataloging-in-Publication Data Pending

For Joseph and Lydia,
the Lights of my life.

"There is no coming to consciousness without pain. People will do anything, no matter how absurd, in order to avoid facing their own Soul. One does not become enlightened by imagining figures of light, but by making the darkness conscious." — C.G. Jung

CONTENTS

Author's Note   1

PART ONE: INTRODUCTION
The Emergence   5
The Chaos Begins   6

PART TWO: THE HELLENE STORIES
The Ascendance of Zeus   15
Themis the Oracle   26
Hera   32
Pandora   51
Aphrodite   63
Demeter   74

PART THREE: THE CELTIC REALM
Celtic Earth   99
Fires of Bealtaine   111
The Eclipse of Awakening   116
Lammas (Lughnasadh)   120
Samhain   129
Imbolc (Brigid's Day)   140

PART FOUR: THE DESCENT

Inanna of Sumer   151

Hadia of En-dor   153

Malleus Maleficarum (Hammer of Witches)   160

Dame Alice Kyteler and Petronilla de Meath   166

The Sol Niger (Dark Sun)   176

PART FIVE: THE INFINITE LIGHT OF ETERNITY

Lilith's Homecoming   183

Moon Dance   189

Readers Guide Book Club Discussion   195

Glossary   199

Reading List   205

Author's Note

THE ARCHETYPE OF THE CRONE originates in 30,000-10,000 B.C.E., when she was revered in ancient cultures as the Great Mother who ruled over birth, death, and rebirth. With the rise of patriarchy, her archetypal and mystical primacy was overridden by male deities. Impossible to quash, the goddess figure reemerged split into three roles: Maiden, Mother, and Crone, the elder woman wisdom figure. Until recent times, the Crone has been the least acknowledged of the archetypes in the world because of her innate power and unwillingness to capitulate to patriarchal norms and social expectations. Hence, older women have been envisaged as ugly and troublesome, and pejoratively called crone, witch, hag, harpy, harridan, battle-axe, scold, bitch, shrew, etc.

In *Behold*, the character of Lilith, "the all-Seeing, all-Knowing Spirit of the Cosmos," reclaims the original nomenclature of Crone to give to the name the kudos and respect that elder wise women (and *all* women) so rightly deserve, and in doing so, offer a new way of Being in the World.

PART ONE

Introduction

The Emergence

In the beginning, when the Infinite Light of Eternity prismed through the Great Darkness, Creation formed Lilith to be the Spirit of the Cosmos. It shaped her Being into an all-Seeing, all-Knowing enigma too vast to comprehend. She became the holder of the Mysteries of Life, Death, and Destruction and the Bringer of Transformation. She dwelled in the deep darkest void, a lustrous pearl in the Eternal Light at its centre, the Light of Truth, the Source of the Soul.

My emergence came later as other goddesses began to take shape in the Cosmos. I arrived under Lilith's wings, a Being of Darkness and Light like her. I am Hekate, Lilith's Messenger and conduit of Divine Wisdom. I am the Light in the silence of the Dark Moon, and the Bringer of Truth.

It was we two Ancient Goddesses who led the way for existence, bringing more and more spiritus for the Soul of Creation to unfold Heart-Soul and Knowing among the spheres. We understood the subtle laws of Temperance, Reciprocity, and Balance. We named the aeon in which we dwelled The Profound Harmony. Over millennia the blissful existence we had to come to cherish had slowly fractured and devolved. And I was about to encounter the chaos that lay beyond the bliss.

The Chaos Begins

"We must keep the patterns of Creation in motion to incarnate our Souls to the highest vibration," Lilith told us Ancients as she drew us together as one. "If not, we will become lost fragments of the whole, eternally frozen in the void. I warn you, the forces of change will wreak havoc in all the Realms and bring chaos to the Harmony. But fear not. Know that through this cataclysm our Souls will rise and transform anew."

"I, too, will play my part in bringing about the changes," I said, hearing a quiver in my voice.

I could not comprehend the depth of Lilith's vision. Yet, I could see the powerful urgency of it burn within her. I dreaded the imminent departure from our blissful Other-world Realm to travel to existences where chaos triumphed. And I was right to.

Throughout the ages, fear of our silent Dark Moon Wisdom and the sacred mysteries at its core had grown like a plague among the gods and mortals. It was Lilith, especially, of whom they were frightened. She had been turned into a daemon of darkness, an object upon which to place their fears and delusions, while hiding from the Truth within themselves. Not that it bothered her. She knew the terrifying power of her primordial presence. She, both Light and Darkness, the Great Mother of All, the Source of existence

I doubt it helped that we laughed in the face of the gods at their grandiosity and pettiness. No one in the realms other than Lilith and me dared remind them of their mediocrity. We would taunt them by throwing their misshapen shadows before them in the moonlight, sights they did not wish to see. They preferred their mirrors of polished gold made to frame themselves to perfection.

Jealous and unnerved by our Ancient Seeing and Knowing, the gods avoided even whispering our names aloud lest they summon our presence. Instead, they'd scratch our symbols in the dust, hissing like snakes as they drew Lilith—a monstrous serpent with enormous outstretched wings; and me with my torches as large as the Cyclopes. In truth, the phosphorus flames of my magnificent torches could have lit the way for them through the Dark Moon to Eternity.

By the time of the Titans and Hellenes, the gods had turned their backs on the path to the Source and the Sacred Power and Wisdom at the centre of Darkness. The ease with which they governed the Realm and amassed their riches led them to believe they had found all the power and wisdom they could ever need. Even the mighty Zeus, bewitched as he once was by me, only yielded to my charms and touched Infinity when in the raptures of lust. I knew he feared inwardly that my dark powers outmatched his own. And he would tolerate no talk of Lilith.

Millennia of such denial took its toll on us.

"We have become the unspeakable ones, expunged since the earliest his-stories of Mesopotamia and Sumer," I said to Lilith as we descended invisibly amongst the Titans and Hellenes. "Have they silenced us forever?"

"Hah!" Lilith laughed. "As if we could be silenced."

Instinctively I knew as she spoke that despite her legendary vision, even she could not foresee what lay ahead. In hindsight it was a blessing neither of us could. It was the Eye of the Fire that awaited us. A Sacred Incubation like no other. These are the tales I must share with you before I venture on, so that you come to know about the past.

Since then, a new aeon has begun to dawn. We are drawing back the blackened veils that have surrounded our Sacred Wisdom. We, the Ancient Seers and Knowers, must show ourselves fully again, for we are being called from near and far as Earth's Seers and Knowers awaken. Their lights are flickering like stardust all over the Earth's orb as they gather to invoke the return of the Sacred Femina, the source of Heart-Soul. Lilith and I, too, are ready.

I, Hekate, Goddess of Death and Rebirth, the Truthbringer of the Infinite Light stand before you. If you wish to save the Earth upon which you stand, and the Cosmos in which you dwell, I bid you accompany me and my torches through the portals of time to the Wisdom of the wondrous Moon. There you will face the Light of Truth, the Eternal diamond hiding in the shadows of your Soul. The path is not easy as my tales will tell, but have no fear. The Light of Truth will set you free.

PART TWO

The Hellene Stories

"Begin the story with our final descent to the Hellenes," Lilith said, drawing a vaporous mist around her like a silken robe. "The tales they carved on stone and scribed for mortals to know of them in times to come."

"But we are rarely named among the gods and goddesses in those tales," I said.

"That may be. And yet mortals need the Hellene tales to see a picture of themselves. For they have lost their way on Earth and forsaken their Truth. They have become the very image of the pantheon's unruly gods."

She was right, of course. Aeons ago she had watched the great Beings of Atlantis as they advanced Earth to its highest vibration. Their crystalline wisdom was unsurpassed. The Atlanteans' Sacred Geometry had connected all things in the Cosmos and painted the Earth in every colour of the spectrum. As they left Earth's portal, their translucent eyes had shone with optimism for the success of mortals' evolution, leaving traces of the Eternal Light behind for all to see.

Attuned to Lilith and me, the ancient mortals who first succeeded them on Earth understood the Laws of Creation and the Wisdom of Nature. They knew Earth would bring forth destruction as well as abundance in the cycle of Creation. They held no judgement or dread of the unseen and unknown. The Blood Mysteries and Inner Wisdom of the Femina that honoured Nature and the rhythmic cycles

11

of the Sacred Moon were worshipped as integral to life. The ancient ones paid homage to the triple Goddess in all of her guises: Maiden, Birth-giver, and Crone. It was She who symbolised the Eternal Connectedness of the cycles of Creation, the bonds between all living creatures, and the Knowing of the thrum of the Earth.

But the indigo Earth, for all its promise, would pose challenges for the mortals who came much later. Ferocious storms, searing droughts, and burning orbs hurtling through the skies would panic the mortals, as anxiety and fear replaced their Knowing assurance in Earth's abundant gifts. They would lose the ancients' trust in Nature's wisdom and a new way of things would emerge. Lilith and I watched as the Red Blood of Fertility twisted and turned over time until it would become the symbol of ever-present Death, not Birth and Rebirth.

I fell into despair as ruthless conquerors, the ones they called heroes and whose bloodlust in battle was a measure of courage, rose to ascendancy within male-kind. By the time of the Titans and the pantheon of the Hellenes, the conqueror myths had long since replaced the Ancient Femina myths. Many femina of the Hellenes colluded in the cause of male-kind. As conquering became the way of things, honour for the Goddess, the Sacred, and the Mystery of Being was all but lost. Little by little, the deep Knowing of the Femina got crushed beneath the conquerors' boots. Without the deep Knowing, Heart-Soul declined along with it. Lilith tried to comfort me, calling this devolution The Era of Divergence.

"The Cosmos must evolve," she would remind me. "The will of the conquerors is playing its part. It is an awakening of the eternal Kairos. Remember, we must all incarnate—as One."

As ever, I did not fully grasp the meaning of her words. Did she condone the Sacred Femina slipping into the aethers, with us two limping behind like beggars, barely able to keep her Wisdom alive? Only a few mortals on Earth, the Knowers, still held her Eternal Sight and Wisdom, passing it on by word-of-mouth. But for most of them, the Sacred Femina, the essence of Being as I knew it, was becoming irrelevant.

"Who among them will emerge to bring Earth into Balance once again?" I asked Lilith. "Surely, you can see?"

She would remain silent to my questions as we watched each successive existence and searched for Knowers who understood the balance and flow of life—the spiralling motion outward to Spirit and inward to Soul. It was the dance of evolution needed by immortals and mortals alike to grow and transform. By the time of the Hellene pantheon, we had waited so long, I had become desperate for any sign of Transformation. And even though she never said as much, I had a hunch Lilith had, too.

Chapter 1

The Ascendance of Zeus

The story of the Hellenes began with Chaos, from whose Being emerged the primeval deities Gaia, Tartarus, and Eros. In an explosive rupture, together with Night and Day and the Heavens and the Cosmos, they created the first order of beings called the Titans. But it was not until the birth of the Titan descendants, the pantheon of the Hellenes, that the prospect of restoring Harmony to the Eternal round shone with promise.

Goddesses from these existences had risen to the challenge of Transformation. But for true Balance to return to the Cosmos, a god of Transformation was needed as well. By the time Zeus appeared on the horizon, Lilith and I had lowered our sights, so that even he offered a glimmer of hope. Lilith and I swept his mother, Rhea, away to Arcadia for safety during her confinement, where the Goddess legacy was still strong. We needed to prevent Zeus from falling prey to the lineage pattern of devouring one's offspring in a jealous and ferocious act of filicide, which had begun with Zeus's grandfather, Ouranos, and was followed by Zeus's father, Kronos. Kronos had watched over Rhea's confinements like a panoptic daemon, quickly engulfing Zeus's five older siblings as soon as they emerged from Rhea's womb, lest they end his reign.

When Zeus came into existence, Rhea quickly gave him to us.

"Do not tell me where you will take him," Rhea said. "Just as long as he is safe there. I am placing my trust in you."

We took him far away to Crete to be raised in anonymity in the Diktean Cave, famed by the Goddesses for its hidden chambers and anonymity. Melissa, the Bee Goddess, and her daughters and nymphs, the Melissaea, cooed and sang to him, feeding him milk from the goat-nymph Amaltheia, mixed with drops of fermented honey to sweeten his nature. They made him a golden cradle of nectar and wax and hung it in a hallowed ash tree between nests of bees so that Kronos could not hear little Zeus cry as we raised him in the soothing hum of the hives. We knew he would never believe Rhea's story that Zeus was a stillborn creation, though she could spin a tale as smooth as a silkworm's cocoon. We suggested she feed Kronos a stone swaddled in cloth to satiate his devouring madness.

We were as vigilant as mountain-hawks over their young as we watched Zeus grow. We sent Metis to teach him the art of deep thought and intuitive knowing. She was a daughter of the Titans Oceanus and Tethys of the Moon, and was the embodiment of fluidity, reflective and deep. But despite all her wisdom, we could see that she was far too soft on him. She and the Melissaea had let him run wild, doing as he pleased. Young Zeus had a constant erection as he grew, a satyr from the start. While we watched and waited, Metis proposed a plan to us. She wanted to create a daughter with him, one who merged traits of both femina and male-kind. We cautiously agreed.

"You must go to him as his first, Hekate," Lilith said as we watched him coveting Metis day and night. "Metis can do her creation with him later. You must tether him and keep in his ear. Let us not forget he is part of Kronos. He is already unbridled enough."

"I will do as you say," I said. "But let us hope he does not degrade and corrupt the Sacred Mystery of Union that I shall teach him into a feverish ecstasy of his own." I added, aware of the tingling from a hazy and distant premonition.

When the time was right, Metis disappeared from the hidden refuge, and the Melissaea flew away. By day, Zeus was frenzied, searching and calling out for them—Metis especially, spilling his seed in the heat of night as he dreamed of her. Slowly, I spun my web around him, entering his dreams as an erotic prophecy, leaving him sleepless, thrashing with feverish desire. When I finally came to him in mortal form, my hair as black as the velvet night, my skin glittering like the Moon on the Aegean, he cried out in fright.

I swathed him in my light and bound him to me, entwining him in the mortal limbs I had conjured. He groaned and shouted as we slowly climbed the hallowed mountain of desire. He wanted to possess me wholly, to spend his own selfish pleasure, but I prolonged his agony until he surrendered to me. He clung to me as he peaked in ecstasy, floating like a feathery wisp into the Infinite Void. Many existences had passed since I had last performed the Sacred Union, and I confess it gave me pleasure. I had almost forgotten the epiphany of it. As I had predicted, he was insatiable. His father's rapacious appetite and Metis's intuitive art had bred exemplary prowess in him. His urge to conquer was unrelenting.

"I will offer you half the earth, and the skies and the seas," he said, "if you will be my wife and stay with me forever. I will honour you above all beings."

I could hear Lilith's laughter ringing in the Cosmos.

"I have been Hekate longer than time itself. I am already in those places," I would explain to him as he stroked my body, laving every curve and dimple of my mortal flesh with his tongue.

"But you have never been my wife," he would argue.

Looking back, all the signs were there. He could not comprehend the notion that I would deny him, nor that there had been many other existences prior to his. He compelled me with his innocence and eagerness, but I saw the impetuous, spoiled child beneath his godly ways. Though my concerns about his allegiance to me were unwarranted, I did not know then that every phantasy of nature he acted out with me—as a bull, a swan, a dove— would later be reenacted by him in the worst of ways.

"I will love and adore you forever," he whispered in my sceptical ear. "I promise you this."

I had powerful reservations about Zeus's suitability for the Balance and Harmony. But there was something about both Kronos and Zeus that had held Lilith's attention.

"Kronos was the first to show great promise since the rise of the conquerors," she said, when I questioned her about it. "Born as he was to Gaia and Ouranus, a son of the Earth and the Heavens, he had the power to reunite. All that wasted potential!"

I could see why her hopes had been so high for him. But Kronos was now as dispensable as the rest, another mere phase in the Eternal Round of existence.

"Then I watched the variations Rhea and Kronos spawned together. Remember, I oversaw the seed of Zeus's creation, I have a vested interest. I am hoping he will be transformative in the Cosmos," she said. "This change requires that male-kind ends the ceaseless quashing of the Sacred Femina that has become a sport for them."

I thought but did not say that Zeus had a propensity for sporting, too, and that the Harmony of all Beings still seemed a long way off. Lilith always heard my thoughts, as if I'd spoken them aloud.

"Do you think I cannot see that?" she said. "You know full well that evolution must take its own path. It is a cocreation in which we are all involved. You are an impatient participant, Hekate."

She would often forget that she was the only one who understood the whole of the evolutionary round. The rest of us, even Ancient me, could only ever see it in parts, like scattered pieces of a timeless puzzle. She could afford to be philosophical back then. But things changed once Zeus had ascended. Change was about to come for Lilith, too, as evolution had spun off its course in ways she had never seen before.

To say that Zeus's return to Delphi wreaked havoc is to understate its impact on us all. Lilith and I had already been too long in the shrouds of our diminished sway. I had continued to rely upon her leadership, and she had overestimated the Hellene pantheon's reverence for her. We had become outsiders in the pantheon, greeted with the hush that attends the arrival of unexpected and unwelcome guests at a jubilant gathering.

"They are mere chaosmos," Lilith would remind me as we watched them teetering on the verge of chaos.

"And it is just the way of things," I learned to respond, knowing those would be her next words.

When we told Zeus that Kronos had engulfed his siblings at birth and had sought to do the same to him, Zeus needed little encouragement to plot his father's ruin. He offered to disguise himself as Kronos's wine-bearer at the Titans' next feast, where he would add a spiritous potion to his drink. Metis helped me concoct the mixture at the potent Full Moon, when the bees of the Melissaea were heavy with syrup. We added juice from poppies the Dryads of the woodlands had brought us. And we gathered the blue-green crystals from inside the rumbling volcanic crater of Aegina, who kept her secret poison hidden there.

On the fated evening, I covered Zeus in a sheen of protection so that even Rhea would not recognise him. The paranoid Kronos was maniacally vigilant, detecting the slightest change in his wife.

"Tell me about the creations that came from Ouranus's blood when my father castrated his own father?" Zeus would ask this every time he saw me.

I had mistakenly seen his frequent requests for the bloodstained story as youthful curiosity, failing to see that a vengeful monster was awakening in him, and that the prospect of the power he would wield after Kronos's demise was more intoxicating to him than I had ever been.

Zeus made his appearance at the Blood Moon Feast, when the reddened heavens lighted our domain, bringing the Moon close to us. It was Lilith's and my special Moon, the femina Moon of the Shape-Shifter. But rather than paying silent homage to the Blood Moon as the Ancients had on this Sacred night, the Titans had a rowdy celebration. They had surrounded themselves with blazing flares (pale imitations of my torches) to ward off unwanted visions, flaunting their wealth by drinking copiously from golden goblets and tossing jewels in the laps of goddesses like spoiled lascivious boys.

"I am tempted to storm into their revelry and extinguish their flares," I said to Lilith as we watched. "How I would love to plunge them into darkness and make them face their shadow selves on this holiest of nights."

She shushed me as Zeus secretly poured the emetic potion into Kronos's wine as planned. He looked on excitedly as it forced the violent expulsion of his swallowed offspring. He had deliberately given his father far more than was necessary, gleeful to see Kronos clutching his throat, his eyes bulging as his face distorted into a Hydra head.

"Who has done this monstrous thing to me?" Kronos shouted between thunderous heaves. "Who dares poison the ruler of all the universes?"

Rhea saw me in the shadows and looked at Kronos with bitter satisfaction. He had denied her and abused her creations. She was not about to cushion his demise.

"Was it you, woman?" his hoarse voice croaked as he looked at her.

"You have forgotten, Kronos, you are not the only power in the heavens," she said.

Rhea's sisters and other Titans and Titanides nodded in agreement as they watched each of Rhea's offspring emerge from his gaping, swollen mouth. One by one, Rhea's creations gathered around her, looking down on the convulsing Kronos with contempt. Zeus shook off his disguise and stepped forward.

"I am Zeus, the last and now first-born son of Rhea and Kronos."

With immaculate timing, Lilith provided an impressive show to remind everyone of her presence. The Cosmos crackled with radiation as lightning ricocheted around the gathering.

"The very heavens welcome me!" Zeus exclaimed, raising his arms as if he were the conductor of the performance.

There was a collective gasp as I stepped out of the shadows, placing a cautionary hand on his shoulder. I wanted him to inspire without the grandiosity that had made the gods malefic. Kronos pointed a spindly finger at me.

"You!" he uttered, before collapsing into a vaporous heap.

Lilith surrounded him in darkness, obscuring him from everyone's view. The three Hesperides, daughters of the violet sunset, drew in the evening stars to twinkle overhead as the music of the spheres spun across the heavens like a thousand strumming harps.

"With our guidance, Zeus will help bring Balance and Harmony to your pantheon," I said, reminding him of his purpose. "There is to be no more rulership by force or fear. We shall once again come to know our Wisdom. The Realm has strayed so far from the Sacred, that Wisdom has been profaned."

The mutterings among the Titans was predictable. They did not understand my words, or the intentions behind them. Atlas, who stood in the midst of the gathering, huffed and snorted.

"Why weren't we consulted about this?" he demanded.

I had taken the liberty of freeing the fearsome Hekatonkheires, the hundred-handed ones, from their imprisonment in Tartarus by Kronos. I had also freed the three, one-eyed Cyclopes, Brontes the thunder, Steropes the lightning, and Arges the brightness. Their show of might and strength was a currency the Titans understood. Zeus cannily called them to his side, as if it were he who had released them from their drudgery. The unalterable change of circumstances now apparent, the grumbling protestors amongst the Titans fell silent.

Lilith and I were aware of Atlas's rancour but were more intent on watching Zeus's siblings as they regrouped.

Hades and Poseidon scuffled briefly for possession of the oceans, but Demeter, Hestia, and Hera happily took their predestined roles. Dearest Hestia, the Sacred Flame of the Hearth and Altar, rose above them all, though few noticed her subtle primacy. Demeter aligned herself with Lilith and me as our third in the lineage of the triple Goddesses. We had decided upon Hera to rule with Zeus as his equal and restore the femina balance to the Hellene legacy. She had the makings of a fierce advocate and was enamoured with him as well.

"He has charisma," she whispered to me, quivering with pleasure as she watched his back muscles rippling while he moved amongst the Titans and lesser gods. The presence of Zeus was more commanding than all his siblings bundled together. The rays of light streaming from his golden aura rivalled the setting sun.

Atlas had moved to the front of the gathering. His towering figure cast a shadow over his fellow Titans. The Cyclopes edged toward him, menacingly flexing their brawn. He watched them from the corner of his eye.

"Let it be heard. I oppose this young nobody Zeus who has come here to overthrow his own father in the foulest of ways and cause ruin for us. And so should you," he said, pointing to the Cyclopes. "So should we all," he added. "We are the almighty Titans."

His voice roared into the aethers like a Cyclopes storm. "And as for you," he said, returning his attention to Zeus as he thrust his finger toward him. "You owe your very inception to us."

Apart from my refusal to be his bride, Zeus had never known a moment of opposition in his existence. So certain of a glorious ascension, he was gobsmacked into silence by Atlas's repudiation. He looked at me, willing me to answer for him.

"She cannot speak for you," Atlas said. "Nor can she speak for us. She, too, is no one, a betrayer to the Titans, a vestige of the forgotten past."

I could feel Lilith's icy hot vapours encircle me, urging me into action. I swept before Atlas as a shadowed mirror, forcing him to look deeply at himself. As we stood face to face, I could see that his stature had deceived him. There was no substance behind his huge facade. He was a mere hollowed-out shell of a Being. If he had been outraged before, when he saw the shadowy transparency of himself, he was furious and spat in the mirror with disgust. I felt compassion for him, but by denying the Truth of his reflection, his fate had been sealed for him that very moment. So, too, had the fate of Zeus.

Themis the Oracle

Ancient Goddess of Divine Law and Order

Before Zeus and his siblings could begin their rule, a decade-long war broke out between them and the Titans at Mount Othrys in Thessaly. Lilith and I had not seen the spark that ignited the Titanomachy, but we had no doubt it came from the spiteful fury of the outraged Atlas. The Titan gods were embittered by the succession of the new generation in the pantheon of the Hellenes, the Olympieions of Mount Olympos. It was all too easy for Atlas to manoeuvre the old guard onto his side.

The Titanomachy marked a prolonged and inglorious time of transition. Deafening claps of thunder, with sudden flares of lightning, resounded mightily through the aethers as the old guard fought ferociously to maintain its sovereignty and the old ways. The new Olympieions were equally determined to sever those ties. Thus, we were all immersed in chaosmos.

Lilith could withstand the tumult, revelling in the changes it wrought. But I vanished to the Otherworld whenever I could, seeking silence and respite there. During my hiatus, the vision of Themis, the Titanide who presided over Ancient Oracles, often appeared before me. She was the voice of Divine Justice and Morality. I knew she would be encouraging them to end the war, to reconcile and pursue good governance. She was the last of them to practise the dying art of Thymos, the Blood-Soul Wisdom of the heart. Without her presence, they would be lost.

Lilith provided the cover of a shielded darkness for me to visit Themis and talk with her. Her sisters, Mnemosyne, Tethys, Theia, and Phoebe sat alongside her. Rhea, Zeus's mother, was conspicuously absent, her allegiance to the Oympieions already apparent.

"Why do you come to me, Hekate? Are you not to blame for this disruption? You and Lilith?"

"It brings me no satisfaction to witness this warfare. It is but a necessary phase in the Transition. I believe you know that better than anyone."

I created a halo of light around us in the dark void in which we sat. Theia stretched her hands to the light as if warming them at the hearth. After a long silence, Themis spoke again.

"What is it you seek?"

"It was you who summoned me through the aether, Themis," I said.

The sisters sat together in front of me shoulder to shoulder and stooped over, waiting for the knell of Truth. It was the shy and inward Tethys who finally gave it voice.

"Is it time to join Zeus and Hera and the others? To leave our own?"

Lilith had been wrong to call me impatient. I had learned long ago to wait for Wisdom to find its own way into the thoughts of others. For some, it never came. But the sisters were miserable, trapped in a wasteland of greed and destruction. The vision of Themis would not have come to me had she not been searching in her heart. She wanted to see the end of the fighting, which meant she had to choose a side. It was a harrowing decision for one who valued fairness above all things.

Themis instinctively placed her hands on her forehead in the sign of dove's wings in flight. It was the symbol of the Eternal Goddess, the Ancient call to the Inner Being. Theia looked at what her sister had done and chuckled softly.

"I see by your hands you have made your decision, Themis," she said.

The language of symbols was truer than the word. Themis had spared herself the pain of speaking of betrayal. All of us let out a sigh of relief. Our meeting had been as taut as a bow with an arrow. I knew they ached at the prospect of leaving their Titan family, but it was to be.

Zeus was inflated beyond all measure by the time Lilith nudged me in his direction again. I had taken my eye off him while seeking refuge from the warring. That had been an error of judgement on my part. Like all wars, a rivalry between two vainglorious fools was at the core of it—the battle was between Zeus and Atlas.

Atlas had never stood a chance, but Zeus in his naivete could not see that. He had wanted to show his mettle, to force victory no matter the cost. And despite Themis having given her wise counsel, Atlas could not let go of the powerful Titanic reins. Bringing Themis into the Olympian fold tipped the scales. When Atlas discovered that she had left, he came and stood at the edge of darkness, shouting at Lilith and me.

"You evil witches, you ugly daughters of darkness! I will hunt you down for all Eternity!"

By now Lilith had endured enough of it. She whacked him with her primordial tail and sent him tumbling like a rock down the slopes of Thessaly. Zeus seized the opportunity to exact his revenge by placing the weighty burdens of the Cosmos on his back.

"You won't be hunting anyone down for Eternity," he said. "Your time is past. You are old, and I am young, and that is the way of it."

Atlas had been ordained as a god of great endurance, but Zeus positioned the burdens high on his back so he would perpetually bow down in subservience. It was an unnecessary corollary to what was already a clear victory. I was increasingly disturbed by Zeus's boastfulness and his penchant for cruelty.

"Pomposity is in his nature," Lilith muttered, watching him over my shoulder as he stood there proudly savouring his victory, the carved muscles on his arms and chest gleaming with sweat.

"He was created during the constellation of the lion. His conquests are a matter of pride. After Crete, you should know," she added. Her wild laughter echoed into the aethers as she vanished, leaving it to me to remind him that true victory came with humility.

"Zeus, look at me," I said, with a scorpion sting in my tone.

"My loveliness," he said, turning to me with his arms wide open, beaming with delight.

"It is not your embrace I seek. You are behaving like a fool. A *young* fool. Atlas was never your foe. He only needed time to release his attachment to power. From this time on, Themis is to be your counsel on fair and abiding governance. Hestia will remind you of the subtleties of the Hearth and the Altar, the art of sitting patiently with both the knowns and the unknowns. For the Paradox of Balance lies therein. The leadership of the Heavens and Earth is divided among you and your siblings. It is not yours alone."

He pouted like the spoiled child that he was, staring into the distance as if pondering the mandate.

"These are not matters for your deliberation. They are decrees," I said, as I shot a blast of fire at him from one of my torches, close enough to singe his beard. He turned his back on me in a show of disdain.

"As you wish," he mumbled.

By the time he turned to face me again, I had disappeared. While speaking with him, my Knowing had revealed with shocking clarity that the Hieros Gamos, the Sacred Union we had once engaged in, had not been sacred to him at all. It had merely awakened yet another kind of greed and lust—predation of the femina. His hidden cruelty stung me like the stab of a knife. Lilith, too, was pained when I told her of it, albeit in her dispassionate way.

"Please do not say, 'It is as it is,'" I said to her. "Despite everything we have done, his existence will be yet another one that takes the Cosmos further away from Balance, from Transformation. He aims to rule over the Infinite for his pursuits alone, not for the sake of Transcendence."

"We must be patient, Hekate. The Hellenes will bring the archetypes of mythos to the fore once again. That is at least some consolation."

"But meantime, I fear they will undo our Sacred web and destroy Divine Femina in the process," I whined, feeling defeated by this wasted opportunity.

And so, as the Olympieion story under Zeus took form, Lilith and I were forced further towards the umbra, the darkest void of darkness. The gods still feared us, it is true, but they had replaced our stories with those of the conquerors to glorify and enshrine themselves. The Great Creatrix, the Goddess and Priestess in every Being, was dead and forgotten, like a corpse left on the battlefield as the conquerors marched on to further victory.

Hera ~ Queen of Olympos

Goddess of Unions, Childbirth, and Family

"We must speak of Hera," Lilith said. "The old stories told of the goddess are tainted with the tellers' bad blood. She was too feisty and fearsome a queen to be remembered justly in the tales of male-kind. Her Truth must be told. She was always one of us."

I thought of the many great achievements in Hera's existence as Queen and wondered where to begin. The story of Jason and the Golden Fleece sprang to mind. Hera had provided safe passage for Jason and the Argonauts to find the Golden Fleece, which would bestow upon him his rightful place as King of Iolcos. But this kind and powerful deed got twisted into a tale of Hera's vengeance against the old Iolcos king. There were so many twisted tales about her, I had lost count.

Lilith sensed my hesitation. "Let us begin with the union she endured with Zeus and the creation of her offspring. The story will unfold from there. She had the allegiance of her sisters and many more allies and friends than the old stories tell."

Not long after the announcement of Hera's pending union with Zeus, she had urgently summoned Lilith and me to meet with her at her temple in Delphi. We both had a sense of foreboding as we approached the gleaming pillars of her temple high on the slopes of Mount Parnassus.

"I no longer desire to unite with Zeus," she said, as we stood before her throne. "I cannot wed someone who holds the Femina in contempt. I have spoken with Hestia and Demeter, and they will support whatever decision I make. The older and wiser Titaness Themis would make him a far better match. She is the Oracle. She can teach him the art of Blood-Soul Wisdom. And she may tolerate his lustful wanderings. I will not."

Hera stood up, her long silken robes trailing behind as she glided out to the open terrace. She gazed at the azure sea, calm and hazy in the shimmering heat.

Lilith sighed and spoke quietly to me. "It will take a fleet of Oracles to harness these creatures. And many aeons more to shift them from their greed for power to knowing the Harmony again."

She went to the terrace door and called to Hera. "Come. We must talk."

Hera returned to the room and slumped against the cushioned seat of her throne. I had only ever seen her sitting upright and proud in its emerald splendour.

"Do not shrink in defeat, Hera," Lilith continued. "Zeus has to be shown how to be in harmony with Femina, with the true Divine. Someone has to tolerate him, to teach him. Someone has to endure the battle of wills with him. You are that one. He does not yet comprehend fidelity. If that is what you seek, release yourself from the union. Either way, you will become known as a Dark Goddess like ourselves. You can choose to play your part or be cast out to the aethers as we have been."

"Why must it be as you say? Is this to be my only choice?" she argued. "He is free to do as he chooses. And I am not?"

Like Zeus, Hera had been created when the Sun travelled through the Leo constellation. She was as headstrong and fiercely independent as he, and not as given to inward thought as Demeter and Hestia. She was his mirror, but with the compassion he sadly lacked.

Lilith lifted her vaporous raiment and cast a cold, dark mist over the Aegean, turning the sea slate grey. The temperature suddenly dropped, as if crystals of ice were about to fall.

"You *are* free, Hera, if you say you are. And you are not, if you say you are not. All are constrained by circumstances yet are free to deal with them as they please. Speak with Hekate. Blessed be."

At that, she instantly vanished into the darkness. The sea and sky returned to hazy blueness, as if Lilith had never been there with us, though I knew she listened from beyond.

"It seems I have been chilled and chastised," Hera said.

We laughed together, knowing it was so. She spoke her thoughts aloud, sighing at each pause.

"What else is there to do but partner this infidel? I know it is my destiny, but I resist being bound to him with every fibre of my Being."

She rested her thumbs on her forehead, splaying her fingers in the sign of the dove. The Wisdom of it calmed her.

"I will play my part. But I will not make it easy for him, nor for the objects of his pleasure if they comply with him and defile the Sacred Femina."

Predictably, preparations for the union of Hera and Zeus would take a crooked path. The date set for the celebration was at the exact point in the ecliptic when the Celestial Spheres stood still. Hera did not engage with Zeus in the time leading up to the celebration. She kept him waiting a whole Moon cycle to align the day of the union with the full Moon when her fertility would be at its peak.

"She is very beautiful, but I do not think she cares for me," Zeus said, as he and I sat together.

The fingertip of a bone-white Moon was just visible on the horizon. I had hoped that the hush of the aethers in the early dawn would open his inward eyes. But Zeus was distracted by the reckless force of sexual desire surging within him, the legacy of his patriarchal line.

"I have been staying away from others to prove my loyalty to Hera, as Hestia suggested," he said.

"Have you shown your interest in ways other than to leer at her?"

He looked at me as if I had quite lost my wits.

"But she knows I am to be joined with her. What other kind of interest need I show?"

I despaired at his blindness. Lilith made her presence known with a sigh of disgust.

"Why is it I displease you both? Am I not the powerful god who led the overthrow of the Titans?"

The puerility of his conqueror mind was more than Lilith could bear. She encircled him in a pelting storm of gritty mist. He bellowed like a beast being speared in the flank. I left him alone to consider the message she had sent. I was weary of guiding him. He drew on my essence like an overgrown babe who won't stop suckling from its mother. Lilith and I watched from afar as he lashed out at the swirling debris, trying to remove the conjuration.

The tormented Zeus escaped to a forest where the birds of the Earth dwelled. There, he found a baby cuckoo alone in a nest. The stinging cloud around him fell away as he scooped the bird up, nest and all, and laid it outside the gates to Hera's domain. While not known for gentle ways like Hestia, she was gentle with her Griffins and the Earthly beasts and birds. Zeus had gifted her a worthy token of his pledge.

The Dryads, the nymphs of the forests, heard the tiny cuckoo's calling first and emerged from the foliage to tend to it. They carried the bird to Hera, who crooned sweetly to it. Zeus, watching from a distance, seized the moment to present himself to her. When she kissed him in her sensual manner to show appreciation for the gift, he mistook it for an invitation. He began groping her wildly, forcefully pulling up her gown, and thrust his erect phallus into her yoni.

"What are you doing!" she shrieked. "The kiss was meant as a thank-you. Are you truly so ignorant?"

"Do you not desire me as much as I do you?" he protested.

"Whether I do or not is of no importance. What matters is that you learn the right way to conduct yourself if you are to be with me. Now go. I will see you at our union—if I decide to wed you at all."

The battle of wills between them was a harbinger of things to come. Zeus stumbled away like the thwarted lover that he was. Hera's imperious gaze followed after him until he faded from sight. I knew she would join with him in the union as planned, but Zeus had failed to win her respect, and in so doing, he no longer ignited the flame of Eros in her.

The day of the union between Hera and Zeus went smoothly enough, although I saw him disappear with Metis, his first true love, during the feasting, and I suspected the outcome. Lilith made an appearance after the sun had set, descending in a cloud of smoke amid the melee. The crowd hushed and gasped when she emerged from the mirage with a great tree laden with golden apples.

The Sacred Tree of Knowledge was no mere gift. The Wisdom that lay in the seeds of its fruit bestowed on the couple the duty of Transforming the Cosmos. Zeus was rendered speechless by the onerous task placed upon them with this gift. But Hera was delighted, seeing it as a promise of hope for their future.

"The tree shall be planted in the Garden of the Hesperides," she announced, "as a reward for them singing so sweetly during the nuptial ceremonies."

"And Ladon, our immortal serpent, shall guard the gift," she commanded, knowing the fearsome creature would wind its sinuous body around the tree's trunk and prevent its golden temptations from being stolen by the undeserving.

In time, the first creation of Zeus and Hera arrived—Ares, an offspring who would inherit the worst traits of his warring male-kind lineage. He was a thunder-tempered child-god with meagre breadth of mind. At the same time, Metis had created a more advanced Being with Zeus, a femina counterpart to Ares in the form of Athena. Even as a youth, she would be swifter and more skilled than Ares, a strategist as well as a just and indomitable warrior, and a new Goddess of the Arts.

Zeus was enraged to learn that Metis had seduced him on the wedding night for the sole purpose of Athena's creation—and worse, that she had consulted with Hera about it before the deed. To save face, he boasted that after devouring Metis, their daughter Athena had sprung from his loins.

Lillith laughed when I told her of his boasts.

"As if he had the makings for such Divine genesis!" she said. "No one but innocent mortals would believe such phantasies."

Without wars to engage in, Zeus had become bored and restless, befriending any god who would listen to his endless shamming.

Hera created a second son, Hephaistos, whose weakness of the legs made him unsuitable for warring. Zeus scorned the child-god for his imperfection. One day when the young god bravely intervened in a fight between his parents, Zeus threw Hephaistos from the top of Mount Olympos, permanently injuring the child. Zeus's assault on their son was the turning point for Hera.

"How dare you!" she yelled at him. "How dare you violate a creation of mine! I will make you suffer for this."

The Olympieions and their minions ducked behind the pillars and statues of the palace hall to witness the fight.

"I am the God of Olympos!" Zeus shouted. "I can do as I please. No child of mine will dare speak against me!"

"He was trying to defend me, you arrogant, ignorant fool. You are as heinous as Kronos," she spat. "I only hope one of your offspring will avenge what you have done to our child."

She wrapped her arms around Hephaistos to protect him from Zeus.

"You will have no more offspring with me," she said. "I will sit on the throne beside you to make sure you govern properly, but *never* will you bed me again."

Lilith and I hovered above them, uncertain whether to intervene. Hera took her son by the hand and swiftly departed. Zeus stood there frozen in astonishment, as if his feet had turned to marble. Her words, overheard by all, had shocked and wounded him, far more than we would have expected. It seemed a just and fitting punishment that he be denied her glorious sensuality and any more legitimate offspring.

Hera took Hephaistos to Lemnos, where he would be safely raised under the care and tutelage of Thetis, Goddess of Water, and the Ancient Titanide, Euronyme. He had shown early promise with his craft-making skill, and although the Sinteis of Lemnos were pirates, they were also master metal forgers. They took the gentle-natured child-god under their wing, teaching him all they knew. He soon surpassed their knowledge and secured his place at Olympos as the most exceptional alchemist and metal forger the pantheon had ever known. Hephaistos was a breath of fresh air for Lilith and me, and his good and decent nature made him the perfect counterweight to the amoral Olympieions. But even he would eventually lose his way.

Meanwhile, Zeus soothed his injured pride by forcing himself on every nymph and mortal he had ever desired. The first of his conquests was the mortal Alcmene, whom he deceived into copulating with him by assuming the shape of her husband Amphitryon. Soon after, Zeus returned to Olympos, boasting that he would give birth to another child, just as he had with Athena. Lilith's laughter at this absurdity echoed across the hills of Olympos. He hated the sound of it, well knowing that some of the Olympieion pantheon would be laughing along with her.

I went to Hera, telling her that giving birth to a half-god, half-mortal creation would be prolonged and painful for Alcmene. Hera, eager to counteract Zeus's every move, went to Alcmene's side immediately, bringing along her trusted midwife Lucinda. When the creation finally emerged, Hera offered to suckle him, knowing the child-god would deplete an already exhausted Alcmene of every resource her body could provide.

"I will bring him back to you every day," Hera said. "We Goddesses know only too well the sorrow of an absent child."

"Then I shall name him Heracles, the glory of Hera," Alcmene said, "as a tribute to you for coming to me with Lucinda and saving the life of myself and my child."

The next of Zeus's offspring was born to the Titan maiden Leto. She was a shy and obliging Titaness, her sweetness reminding him of Melissa, the honeybee goddess who had helped raise him. Leto's parents, Phoebe and Coeus, had guarded her vigilantly, aware that Zeus had been watching her while she bathed. Yet clever Zeus found a way to distract them by getting Ekho, an Oread mountain nymph, to talk endlessly to us all while he carried out his seduction with Leto.

Phoebe and Coeus were incensed by his flagrant disregard and sought me out, looking to hide their pending grandchild from the undeserving Zeus. I knew Hera would see to their wishes.

"Can you call on Boreas, the North Wind, to speed Leto away?" she asked me. "I think the Isle of Delos would be the perfect place."

Isolated and barren Delos was indeed an ideal place to hide a child. The soaring cliffs of the mountainous isle rose forbiddingly from the sea to the summit. It looked impenetrable to unknowing eyes. The caves of Delos were familiar only to the Gaian Priestesses, the most Ancient of Knowers.

Hera, Demeter, Hestia, and I joined Leto for her gestation, as did Metis. The Nereids, the many-numbered sea nymphs, joined us, too, along with the Oceanids, the ocean nymphs, bringing their divine blessings to answer Leto's every hope and dream for her offspring.

Leto's creations, the twins Artemis and Apollo, shone like mirrors of the sun and moon from their very inception. Artemis came first, her skin pale as molten silver. The young goddess was fleet-footed as soon as her toes touched the ground. Golden-skinned Apollo followed, his voice as pure as the bells of Paradise.

On hearing of the plight of Leto, Hephaistos sent a pair of bows and quivers with glowing arrows specially crafted for his stepsiblings. Hera wept when she saw them.

"My clever, wonderful son," she said, as she held the gifts up to the Cosmos and prayed for Lilith's protection over them. "With your help, Hekate and Lilith, Artemis and Apollo will become the most revered of hunters. And they will protect you, Leto, like no other. That is my promise to you."

The next creation of Zeus was made with the beautiful midwife, Maia. I had warned her that Zeus was running wild, taking whoever sparked his desire.

"I shall retreat to my cave on the west face of Mount Cyllene," she said. "No one knows I go there."

Being the oldest of the seven dark-eyed Pleiades sisters meant that her nightly duties took her away from her secret cave. Her departures made her vulnerable. Sure enough, Zeus followed her one evening after bribing his acolytes to ply her with the poppy juice he had stolen from the Dryads. Later, he crept into her cave, seducing her while she lay in a dreamy state of surrender.

"I am more distressed by his deception than by the pending creation," Maia told me. "What is wrong with him? He knows me well enough to have asked. Had he gone about things in the way of a lover instead of a hollow-hearted rapist, I could have discussed it with Hera, too. Not that I wished to couple with him, but at least I would have had a choice."

I relayed the conversation, word for word, to Hera.

"He is punishing me with all of these violations of his," Hera said, curling her hands into fists. "He is a stigma to all of us on Mount Olympos."

"He abuses his position by subjugating the femina around him. In doing so, he destroys the Wisdom of Truth in himself," I said quietly.

"Do not be philosophical about him, Hekate. There is no Wisdom left in him. He is nothing but a brute and a violator. You and Lilith should dispose of him."

I stayed silent at Hera's scolding. I felt wretched enough as it was about Zeus's desecration of the Sacred Union, more than Hera could possibly have known. I sorely regretted showing him the power of Infinity in the ecstasy of our union. He had failed to see it was his surrender to the Light within him that held the key, not his urge to conquer me.

Hera and her sisters and I were present when Maia's son emerged from her womb. We had begun referring to ourselves as "The Midwives of the Heavens" rather than Moon Goddesses, such was the denigration of our Moon Wisdom. It was our way of having the last laugh, since midwifery was at the very heart of the Eternal Round. The

Transformative Life, Death, and Rebirth Transitions would always be our dominion.

"I shall name him after you, Hera," Maia said, as we gathered around her for the birth blessing. "I shall name him Hermes."

Hermes was a precocious child who quickly grew into a trickster, full of jokes and mischief. He became a favourite of the pantheon, as did Zeus's final offspring, Dionysus. Dionysus was the son of Semele, a mortal from the region of Lydia, whose parents, Cadmus and Harmonia, were frequent guests at Olympos.

The entire pantheon had witnessed Semele take Zeus's breath away the very first time he saw her. There she stood, tiny and perfect, like a yellow goldfinch sheltered behind her parents. I had seen Alcmene's gestation and birth agonies firsthand and did not want to witness them again. The statuesque Alcmene was physically strong, like a mountain eagle. Tiny Semele would not birth the child of a god without it ending her own existence. Cadmus and Harmonia summoned me, seeking my advice.

"Please understand, we do not wish to give offence to Zeus, but we do not believe he is a suitable match for our Semele," Harmonia said.

"Besides, he is already joined with Hera," she added. "We do not want him to break his vows to her."

"We beg of you, please watch over her—you and Lilith," Cadmus whispered, fearful of the ears in Olympos hearing Lilith's name.

No one ever spoke Lilith's name aloud, let alone requested her intervention anymore. I had to be honest with them.

"We will do everything we can in our domains, though as you know, we are more restricted than in times past."

We all knew, too, that the harder it was to obtain his prey, the more Zeus would pursue her, and the more treachery there would be until he had prevailed. The many ways in which he and his brothers Poseidon and Hades had found to take their pleasure with unwilling women was acutely distressing to Lilith and me. Their collective power had made them unassailable, beyond the reach of Themis's just governance to whose edicts they paid only lip service.

"He is born of the lineage of unseeing male-kind. Do you remember Amun-Ra? I believe the beginning of it was with the Egyptian," Lilith said, her voice rising out of the darkness. "The Sacredness of Divine Femina is lost on them. Until one is created among male-kind who holds within him the Knowing of this Wisdom, we too will fade from view."

I had never heard such grave talk from Lilith. And never had she spoken such words before mortals. The very idea that the Great Goddess of Darkness, from whom Transformation arose, might be lost left Cadmus and Harmonia shaking with fear for their daughter. But Lilith had already foreseen the imminent death of Semele upon giving birth to her son, Dionysus.

Hera was inconsolable, not only because Zeus had seduced the most innocent of mortals in Semele, but also because of the lies he told to cover up his murderous cruelty. At first, he claimed her death was her own doing, as Semele had begged to see a show of his thunderbolts and lightning. Then he claimed it Hera's fault, that in a jealous rage she had gone to Semele and told her to ask Zeus to show her his powers. Poor Hera had not even known about Semele. She had been busy plotting a scheme with Hephaistos to craft a special throne to trap Zeus and prevent his violating behaviour.

It was I who had gone to Semele disguised as a nursemaid and pleaded with her to beware of Zeus's tricks and manoeuvres. The poor girl was naïve—blank as a new star. Her sheltering parents had told her nothing of the Hieros Gamos. She was wide-eyed as I spoke of it. I knew then what Lilith had seen, that she would perish giving birth to her creation.

Hera continued in her bold opposition to Zeus. But Lilith and I were losing our power to uphold Transformation in the Cosmos. Goddesses and nymphs still favoured us, but like the mortals, they did so quietly in hidden places where we, too, resorted for safety. Apart from appearing in the niches of symbols and dreams, our influence in the Hellenic realm was waning.

While matters of midwifery and the nurturing of new creations had been taking place, Hera and I had taken our focus off Zeus, mostly in disgust. In our absence, he had befriended the young Titan Prometheus. They entertained themselves with Zeus's latest diversion—watching the innocent mortals. Amused by their limitations, Zeus slapped his knee and laughed raucously at their mistakes.

Prometheus, unlike Zeus, felt sympathy for the mortals. He was enchanted by their simple ways.

"Themis once told me that it was Lilith's idea to seed the mortals as part of evolution," Prometheus said.

"Lilith had nothing to do with it," Zeus snorted. "My creation Athena breathed life into them, but it was you and me, my good friend, who modelled them from the clay of the Earth."

Prometheus overlooked Zeus's claim, knowing his manner of telling stories was his way to inflate his esteem.

"They need fire to keep them warm, Zeus. And they need fire to forge pots to cook their food," Prometheus said.

"They will never have fire!" Zeus shouted into the aethers for all of Olympos to hear. "If we give them the power of fire, they will think they are gods, they will think they are just like us. Never. Never. Never! Do you hear me?"

Prometheus grimaced and looked away, not wanting to fall out of favour with his new friend. But each day, as he watched the mortals struggling, he became more convinced of the necessity of helping them. He pitied their vulnerable plight and had fallen in love with their innocence and desperately wanted to be part of their world. He whispered in Themis's ear that he had devised a plan. He would steal a spark of the Divine fire from Hephaistos's forge at night while everyone feasted. Themis promptly summoned Lilith and me.

"Dear Prometheus has told me a plan of which I approve. He wishes to bring fire to the mortals to further their well-being. It is an act of Divine intervention. Can you give him safe passage to complete the task?"

"I shall provide a night webbed in darkness for Prometheus to do the deed," Lilith said, knowing she spoke approval on behalf of us both.

The three of us watched from afar as Prometheus reached Hephaistos's domain. He hesitated at the massive forge guarded by the Cyclopes who slept alongside it, deciding how best to navigate the danger. He tiptoed past them with the stealth of a seasoned thief, his shadowy silhouette flickering in the firelight. He placed a glowing ember in a fennel stalk and nursed its glow as he left the forge and descended to Earth. The mortals were enraptured with the gift, and soon their settlements were alight with warming fires at night.

When Zeus learned of Prometheus's defiant thievery, he stomped and raged, forcing everyone to flee to safety as rocks thundered from the peaks of Mount Olympos. He was inconsolable. Not even poppy juice could conquer the sting of his friend's betrayal. In his agitated state, firestorms shot into the aethers, putting the whole Cosmos at risk. Lilith and I knew that the only ones who could calm him were Metis and me.

He was dishevelled and bleary-eyed when we came to him, lying in a giant nest of empty poppy juice vials.

"My most beautiful goddesses," he slurred as we approached him. "Come, come to me. I shall have you both at once. It has always been my dream."

I wanted to open a portal to the Netherworld and send him there for all Eternity. Lilith nudged me forward. I had brought with me a balsam of dried aconite mixed with nectar to ward off his stupor. He pawed me with his clumsy, gluttonous hands as I administered the potion. Suddenly panicking, he choked and spit it out, fearing he was getting the poisonous emetic that had delivered Kronos to his death. I conjured the soothing hum of the Melissaea, the beloved bee guardians of his childhood. The vision pacified him long enough to get him to swallow it all.

Metis and I stood over him, stern and unyielding. He cowered at the sight of us when he regained his senses.

"He betrayed me!" he cried. "Prometheus has betrayed me!"

"Just as you have betrayed Hera," Metis said. "And so many others."

He had become so accustomed to adoration and pandering that he looked at us in disbelief, as if we were strangers speaking strange words. He tried to turn away from me, but I was too swift for him. Wherever he turned, there I was in front of him, a cold mirror reflecting his petulance.

"Prometheus showed compassion and forethought for the mortals," I said. "His act of courage as a bearer of the Light was ripe with Wisdom for you. Instead, you wallow in self-pity, suffering needlessly, and create suffering around you. If you had any humility, you'd ask Lilith or me to help you find the Light of Truth in yourself."

"Hera banned me from her bed. What was I to do?" he said, playing the victim. "Deny my godly seed from being planted elsewhere? Deny all other women? Starve myself of pleasure?"

He laughed maniacally at the prospect. I wished for Lilith to return him to the dark aethers forever. I knew she would not, though I felt the temptation skim over her, too.

"It had nothing to do with Hera holding you to account. You behave as if you own the mortals and all the other Beings, as if they are mere playthings," I said.

"And your betrayal was not only dallying with the Beings Hera knew about," Metis added. "There was Electra, Taygete, Dana, Leda, Callisto, and the beautiful young Trojan boy, Ganymede...and all the others."

Lilith had come to join the conversation and sat down opposite him. In her presence, his stature diminished to the size of a grain of sand. No longer could he hide the many faces of his duplicity, which were now visible to all of Olympos.

"By your actions, you have given permission to all male-kind to behave as you do," Lilith said. "You have utterly failed to be what you might have been, a Being who shines with the Integrity and Wisdom of the Infinite Light within you."

He flinched as the diamond-sharp blades of Truth she spoke cut into him. In a fleeting moment, he saw who he had become.

"I did not know, I did not know..." he blubbered in self-pity, sending salty torrents of tears down the slopes of Mount Olympos.

Lilith disappeared, and Metis and I left, too, indifferent to his suffering. We knew his remorse would be short-lived. But without us constantly overseeing him, his bruised pride quickly turned to vengeance.

Pandora

The Created Woman

Zeus had banished Prometheus from Olympos and barred him from ever returning. The banishment was like a blessing for Prometheus. He spent his days on Earth with the mortals teaching them how to forge metal into pots and vessels as Hephaistos had taught him. But his contentment was overshadowed by dread. Deep inside, fear gnawed at him like a mortal dog at its bone. He knew the simple act of banishment would not be enough for Zeus. It was the clever idea of the scheming sycophant Hermes that was to be his undoing.

"Could you not punish Prometheus by doing some trickery on his brother, Epithemeus?" Hermes said to Zeus as they sat together one day.

Epithemeus, the more idealistic of the two good-natured brothers, had let it be known in the pantheon that he wanted to marry someone as beautiful as Hera. The gods laughed behind his back at his high-flown hopes. Hermes saw in it a perfect ploy with which to play a prank on the two brothers.

Zeus straightened himself in his throne. The idea had whet his appetite for revenge.

"Pray, tell me more," he said.

"Why not commission Hephaistos to create this dream woman Epithemeus seeks?" Hermes said. "After all, it was his forge from which Prometheus stole the flame. You could trick the creation he makes into punishing them both. I'd call it the perfect retribution."

"We are the cleverest of all the Gods," Zeus said, gloating, his laughter resounding over Olympos.

When they summoned for the work to be done, Zeus and Hermes, of course, said nothing to Hephaistos about their intention for the fate of the creation. Hephaistos spent many a Moon cycle tenderly shaping the femina form as he dreamed her into being. He drew on all the attributes he most admired in the Goddesses on Olympos: Hera's nobility, Demeter's wisdom, Hestia's nurturing, Athena's artistry, Artemis's skills, and Persephone's softness. He would make her hair of the finest spun silver, and the skin of her moulded limbs would be as smooth as treacle honey. Every day, as he toiled at his creation, her lovely face gladdened his heart.

At last came the happy moment to bring the creation to life. He poured liquid gold into the mould he had made and put his precious work into the forge. Then he pulled her out of the flames in great excitement and stood her up in the light to polish her to perfection.

The Cyclopes walked round and round her in wonder. "What name will you give her?" they asked. "What name could befit one so beautiful?"

"I shall name my daughter Pandora, the Being of many gifts," he said.

As the Ancient Midwife of the pantheon, I had come to witness the birth of his masterful creation. "You have forged a masterpiece, Hephaistos," I said, seeing the love for her that shone in his eyes. She was the epitome of all he had dreamed. Not for a moment did I suspect Pandora's existence was part of Zeus's vengeful scheme. Nor did Hephaistos.

Like a proud new father, he held Pandora close beside him as he took her to meet Zeus. Pandora's hazel-flecked eyes widened when she beheld the grandeur of Olympos Palace. Zeus stepped forward to greet her as she entered the hall. She curtsied gracefully, and he clapped his hands in thunderous delight, declaring her perfect, and commanded a celebration. His acolytes swarmed around her like fish in the ocean shoals, nuzzling at her long, silver-white hair and honeyed limbs. Pandora was elated to inspire such adoration, and eagerly consented to everything she was bid to do.

Zeus invited everyone on Olympos to the feast, including Epithemeus and his beloved brother, the suspicious and deeply wary Prometheus.

"Why have you asked me to the feast, Zeus?" Prometheus said, standing before him. "I thought I was barred from Olympos forever? What fate do you have in store for me?"

Zeus turned his head away. Hermes answered for him.

"Go and be seated, Prometheus. It would not do to ask such questions and make a fuss in your situation."

Try as he may, Prometheus could not penetrate the Truth behind his invitation to the gathering. The only ones who would have seen through the charade were Lilith and me, and as ever, we were not invited. It was Hera who summoned me in stealth, sending the sign of the dove's wings into the aether.

When I arrived, I moved beyond the vision of those assembled in the hall, blending like dust into the stone pillars behind the feast table. I watched and waited for the inevitable act of malice.

During the feast time, Hermes stood up to make an announcement.

"We have here today the perfect partner for a certain Titan who wishes to marry one as beautiful as you, Hera—were it possible."

I watched Prometheus blanch, fearing the worst for his brother as Hermes slipped out of the room.

"Something nasty is afoot," Hera whispered to Demeter and Hestia, who sat to her left at the Great Table. "I know my husband only too well."

"Epithemeus!" Hermes called out, as he entered the room with Pandora on his arm. "Come and meet your intended bride, the truly celestial Pandora."

Gasps of wonder filled the palace hall at the sight of her. Epithemeus rose from his seat and walked toward her as if lost in a daze. In that instant, it was clear that he had been duped into playing a part in Zeus's act of revenge.

Seeing what was about to take place, Hera sprang up from her seat and stood in front of Hermes, gesturing for everyone to sit down.

"Gods and Goddesses assembled here, let us welcome Pandora to our realm and bestow gifts upon the couple this very day. Every new union needs blessings—not least, this coupling that seems so well designed."

She smiled like a viper at Hermes and Zeus as she made the edict, both of whom lowered their guilty eyes. But little did she realise that in her wily show of generosity, she had unwittingly fallen into the trap Zeus had prepared for her.

The Gods and Goddesses made grand gestures with their gifts: music to soothe away troubled times, persuasion to remedy arguments, a happy hearth from Hestia. Hermes gave them the gift of curiosity with which to discover all there is to know.

Demeter, Hestia, Hera and I watched anxiously throughout the proceedings, waiting for the details of the chicanery to be revealed. Finally, every gift had been offered but one. Zeus ordered his acolytes to place his gift in front of Pandora. It was a pithos, a large lidded urn carved from clay and threaded with silver and gold, covered in lustrous gleaming jewels— sapphires, rubies, emeralds as large as eggs. Awestruck, the gathering was hushed in silence. Pandora wept at its magnificence.

"But what is in it?" Epithemeus asked.

"Ah," Zeus said. "It is for Pandora to solve that mystery. Hermes has bestowed curiosity upon you my dear, so that you may come to know the secrets of the Cosmos. I wonder which of them lies hidden within. Pray, discover for yourself."

Pandora looked puzzled. I saw her innocent mind spinning with possibilities.

"There is only one condition," Zeus said. "Do not open the lid until you are quite certain about the treasure that awaits you."

"Oh!" Pandora said, clasping her hands together under her chin like an enchanted child. "A mystery!"

No one assembled, including me, knew what Zeus's gift contained, though the artifice of the speech that had accompanied its presentation was clear as day. Prometheus whispered to Epithemeus, urging him to get rid of it.

"I cannot do as you ask," Epithemeus argued. "Pandora may never forgive me. Only look how she adores it. And Zeus would take it as an insult. I do not want to be at the mercy of his vile temper. It is bad enough waiting to see what he will do next to you, Prometheus."

"That is what I am trying to tell you, my brother," Prometheus countered. "We believe it is a trap of sorts, aimed to punish me."

At that, I swiftly made myself visible, so as to urge Epithemeus to follow his Wisdom rather than his starry-eyed desires. But despite our protests, I could see that our words were wasted on him.

Meanwhile, the treacherous Hermes, having eavesdropped on our discussion, rushed to Zeus to make him wise to our talk. Zeus was outraged.

"So, Prometheus has sought Hekate, and no doubt the dark one, to try and hinder me. Two betrayals from him are two too many."

Zeus backed away from me as he spoke and slipped into the throng among the guests. He was beyond the range of my magic, but I could hear him whispering to Hermes.

"Keep him here on Olympos until Pandora opens the pithos," he said. "I wager it will be soon. This time, I will exact so vile a punishment for him that no God, Titan, or mortal will ever dare cross me again. That includes the dark one."

I scoffed at his show of belligerence, little knowing his plan was far worse than anything I could have imagined. As it turned out, Pandora succumbed to the seduction of the sealed pithos that very night. She sent Epithemeus to get more of the ambrosia she had enjoyed at the feast. While he was gone, she poked and prodded at the waxed cover, hoping for a peep inside. But it would not yield. She spied Epithemeus's knife laying on a table and fetched it to dig underneath the wax, gently prying off the lid.

The force of the explosion from its unsealing threw her across the room. She sat in dazed shock and watched as a plague of sorrows surged from the urn and whirled about the room like one of Lilith's castings. Out flew the most mutant and primitive forms known to existence, wildly searching for innocent mortal beings in which to insert themselves. Misery, Want, Deceit, Violence, and Sickness whistled past her; demonic apparitions of every conceivable form of malevolence and madness raced to the Earth. Pandora ran over to the jar and slammed the lid, trapping the last of the descendants inside it, the one known as Elpis. Its role was to breed hopelessness in mortals. Trapping Elpis, she had assured the mortals one last vestige of innocence—hope for their future.

Epithemeus returned to Pandora's side, and when he saw what she had done, he keened in agony along with her. Not only had he and Pandora been played like fools, the innocent mortals his dear brother Prometheus so loved were now scarred with the worst traits in all of the Cosmos.

When Hermes announced what had happened, the tragic news broke Prometheus's will to live, just as Zeus had hoped. The mortals that Prometheus cherished with all his heart had been contaminated, their sweet purity lost forever. He barely protested when Zeus made a decree to have him chained to a rock, commanding vultures to tear at his liver each day, only for it to regenerate again by night. By the time I found him, he was draped over the rock like an empty sack, utterly abandoned to the living death.

"My dear Prometheus, I am so sorry," I said, wiping his brow.

As I drove away the savage vultures with my torches, Lilith appeared, the icy burn of her presence was a welcome relief to us both.

"No need to ask whose work this is," she sighed with disgust.

She cast her magic over his gaping side, sending the Light of the Cosmos to heal the wound and seal the flesh with a scar, making him impenetrable to the vultures.

"Prometheus, you were a friend to the mortals without equal among the gods. You were the only one in the pantheon who took a genuine interest in them and showed Compassion. In amongst the woes that have now befallen them, they have at least learned Compassion from you. And without Elpis adding his evil to their woes, they will yet have hope for their future."

He whispered a faint thank you.

"Furthermore, you taught them the skills of survival. To be creators on the Earth, they needed those. They need the challenges the woes will present them. It will make them grow from innocence into Knowing. They have the wondrous orb of Earth and its bounty to protect. All is as it is meant to be."

Having said her piece, Lilith vanished in a swirl of blue vapour. Prometheus stood upright again, blinking his eyes as if awaking from a dream. I put my torches on his chains, incinerating them into flakes of soot. He looked down at his freed wrists and ankles, and rubbed his hand over the scar on his side, astonished to be liberated from the nightmare of his punishment.

"I fear Zeus will return to exact more pain when he hears of this," he said.

"Now that he has done his worst, he will be satisfied. I will tell him it was Heracles, his current favourite son, that unchained you. Heracles will agree to it. He owes me a favour of great magnitude. I suggested that he send Atlas, Zeus's sworn enemy, to retrieve a coveted golden apple so that Heracles could complete his twelve labours. And it was I who told Ladon the serpent to allow it. Zeus will trust the conquering Heracles to be acting heroically on your behalf."

"Never can I thank you enough, Hekate. It is a pity no one knows of the kindhearted and righteous deeds you do."

"Perhaps I would not be so feared if they did," I laughed. "My existence and what I do in the realms are tied with the eternally impartial Lilith. And as she says, all is as it is meant to be."

As I flew up to the heavens and Prometheus's lonely form faded into the distance, I pondered on what had come to pass. If Lilith and I had thought Zeus rapacious and cruel, the revenge he had exacted on Prometheus took him to the depths of corruption.

"At last, Lilith," I said having summoned her from afar. "Zeus descending to such debasement is the sign this existence in its decline."

"It is now our role to ensure that the Greater Laws of Evolution intervene," she said. "Then a new way of Knowing and Being can emerge through the Cosmos."

With that in view, Lilith and I decided it was time to pay Zeus another visit. She cloaked Olympos in an avalanche of night so dark and thick it was hard to breathe. We appeared in front of Zeus as he snored on his throne, saliva dribbling down his beard. I lit one of my torches, startling him awake. He trembled with terror as Lilith towered over him in a suffocating cloud of smoke.

"We have seen Prometheus," she said.

It was all she needed to say. He fell from his throne onto his knees and covered his face with his hands.

"He is fr- free now," he stuttered, peering through his fingers.

"Heracles freed him, not you," I said.

"It matters little who freed him," Lilith said. "What matters is that you would do such a thing at all."

"I have lost my mind," he pleaded. "Do you not see that—in all the deeds I have done? Ruling has made a madness grow in me. The whole of the pantheon was losing respect. I had to do something bold."

We said nothing. Our chilling silence roared in his head like the winds of a mighty tempest. He wrapped his arms over his head to cover his ears.

"I have wronged you!" he cried. "Forgive me, I have so grievously wronged you and the whole of the pantheon."

Lilith and I may have been unmentionables—dark ones in the Hellene world. But we were still the bearers of the Light of Truth in the face of foul play and self-deceit. Zeus started to whimper like a beast in its death throes, aware that he had long since lost any trace of decency. There was no Light left in him. Like so many before him, he grew emboldened and blinded by wielding so much power, and he had been sheltered from its repercussions.

"You will show repentance before your existence ends," Lilith said. "We shall be watching. And waiting. Time has nearly run out for you. Make good use of it."

It was Hera who delivered the news to us of Zeus's pledge to redeem himself. "He has asked if we might renew our union to show his remorse. He said the ritual would be a fitting tribute to me and all the femina," she laughed. "I scorned his offer, of course. He will not change. But I have made him apologise to everyone he has taken against their will."

Themis had been sitting with Metis and me when Hera arrived to share the news. I waited for Themis to speak in her role as Oracle.

"Hera, if you see fit to give your consent, the pantheon would benefit from the ritual as a show of stability. This era has grown as unruly and corrupt as the days of the Titans. Zeus has been reminded of his godly role by Lilith.

Let us see if he can meet this final challenge and have a surge of growth before his death knell strikes."

And so, preparations for the reunion of Hera and Zeus commenced. But in keeping with the traditions of mythos, it would herald yet another chain of events.

Aphrodite

Goddess of Love and War

The whisperings on Olympos alerted me to the forth-coming arrival of a surprise visitor. Her familiar scent of smouldering labdanum and aloewood resins, sweetened with nectar, wafted on the breezes. Even before I emerged at the palace, I could envisage the clamouring entourage trailing behind her.

She was an Ancient Goddess, nearly as old as myself. I had known her as Astarte in Phoenicia and Ishtar in Babylonia. She was the Goddess of War and its antithesis, Love—the blind twins of passion. I wondered what she would look like this time. She recreated herself in every existence with a different face. The one thing that remained constant was the collective gasp she drew for her beauty. The visage she chose was always seductive and mes-merising to male-kind. She excelled at playing the temptress. I wondered if Lilith had woven her magic to bring this goddess into the fold.

She glided toward the banquet hall with many gods and goddesses of the pantheon drifting behind her, as if caught in a spell. Her gown was diaphanous as always; her full, pale breasts stood out proudly on her chest, and her firm buttocks blushed pink. The cord drawn tightly around her waist carved her shape to perfection.

Wide-eyed and slack-jawed, Zeus stood up from his throne when she entered the hall. Hera remained seated, with the faintest of smiles on her face. I could see it was she, not Lilith, who had called forth this goddess as a test for Zeus before their reunion. Throughout the aeons, male-kind had fallen prey to her power.

"I am Aphrodite," she said, extending her soft lily of a hand to Zeus.

Dumbfounded, he first put out one hand, then the other, looking as confused as on the night I first came to him. It took all my effort to stifle my laughter. I sensed Lilith beside me, chuckling to herself.

Hera rose and stepped forward. She greeted Aphrodite with the sign of the Goddess, which befuddled Zeus all the more.

"You two know one another?" he said, surprised.

"Zeus, dear husband, how could you not know of the marvellous Aphrodite?"

He looked from one Goddess to the other in disbelief, as if poppy juice had clouded his sight. It was too soon after his brush with Lilith for him to return to his old ways. But he puffed out his chest and began preening himself as he paced back and forth like a caged lion.

Hera revelled in her moment of triumph. The pantheon had all witnessed her husband's restraint in the face of a powerful seduction. On the crest of her success, she had failed to see the trouble looming in the wings. Her sons Ares and Hephaistos lurched toward Aphrodite like a pair of bumbling drunks. Ares pushed Hephaistos out of the way, making him stumble and fall a step behind. Hera's grand victory shattered at that instant. Zeus had not succumbed to the temptation, but it was clear to Hera and all assembled that winning the hand of Aphrodite was now to be a contest between her two sons.

"These handsome gods must surely be your sons?" Aphrodite said to Zeus, waiting until they were in front of her to greet them.

Zeus introduced Ares first, lauding his valour in battle; then Hephaistos, praising his skills at the forge.

Hera meekly returned to her seat, silent and ashen-faced, as if felled by an unseen ax.

"Why did Hera not consult us first?" Lilith whispered in my ear. "We would have foreseen this in the blink of an eye."

She stilled the Cosmos around Olympos so that Hera could gather her thoughts and be saved from the devastating loss of face.

"Stand and take your place as ruler," I whispered in Hera's ear. "You are the Queen here, not Aphrodite."

Lilith surrounded Hera in a sphere of brilliant light as she took her place before them. I had never seen her look more radiant.

"Aphrodite," she said. "It seems you have ensnared the hearts of both of my beloved sons."

Hera looked at the two of them; their eyes were glazed over with lust. Zeus was struggling to hide his erection.

"Since choosing a suitor would be a task beyond the power even of someone of your Ancient years," she said to Aphrodite, "I shall make the choice for you."

The crowd chattered with excitement.

"Quiet!" Hera commanded to the pantheon. "Do you wish to hear my choice or not?"

Lilith revealed her presence at that precise moment, standing beside Hera as a show of support. The crowd froze as if stricken by a sudden paralysis.

"Ares travels far and wide in his role as battalion leader," Hera said, "and I dare say he will meet other ripened beauties like Aphrodite. But Hephaistos must remain on Olympos to create his magnificent work. He has little opportunity to meet a suitable partner. Therefore, it is Hephaistos with whom you shall be betrothed."

Her words struck her victim with the sting of a snakebite; it was an outstanding recovery on Hera's part. With a glint of satisfaction in her eyes, she noted Aphrodite's obvious disappointment. In turn, Aphrodite looked around at the lascivious eyes feasting upon her. She had never favoured fidelity in any of her incarnations. She desired the attentions of vigorous male-kind whose lusty appetites could match her own. The lean and limping Hephaistos with his gentle ways was not at all to her taste. Hera raised her arm to subdue the crowd again.

"We shall have a double union," Hera declared. "Hephaistos and Aphrodite shall be joined together along with we two," she said, linking her arm through Zeus's. "It shall be a truly exalted day for us all."

I turned to Lilith, who drew close beside me and disguised us from view while we communed.

"You need to intervene with these immortals," I said to her. "Hera tries in vain to Transform and restore Harmony, while the gods move farther down the path to destruction."

"It is the way of things, Hekate. We can cast magic wherever we like, but if the recipients are not open to the portals, they will not see the Truth of what is there in front of them."

"But what if the mortals follow the lead of these Olympieions and behave like this, too?"

I chanced a look at her, wanting to understand the Cosmos from her celestial viewpoint. It was plain from her face that none of it mattered to Lilith, for whom time had no import. The pantheon and its dramas, the tiny mortals and their quests—to Lilith, they were but gases in perpetual motion and flux.

"It is your destiny to show the mortals the diamond of Light in their shadows, Hekate. They have opportunities to find Wisdom in their dreams and imaginings. In the end, when they stand before me, they will see whether they furthered Evolution or were but passing flickers in the Eternal Round."

"If they become like the gods in the pantheon, they will do anything to avoid the Truth of their hidden selves," I said as I watched them absorbed in their games and vainglory. "None of them wants to cast an eye on the Truth and see their folly."

"But deep in their Souls the mortals will always remember the Dark and the Light from whence they came," she replied, unexpectedly wistful.

She comforted me in her Lilith way, patting me on the head with a whirl of burning ice, before vanishing again.

The garish celebratory feast was soon under way. Hera and Aphrodite sat at opposite ends of the banquet table. Hephaistos raised his glass to toast his bride-to-be at every opportunity. Ares and Aphrodite, meanwhile, might as well have copulated in front of the audience, so palpable was their craving for each other. Zeus watched them greedily, licking his lips and fondling himself under the table.

"Put your tongue and your phallus away," I said to him. "You look like a mortal boy anticipating his first coitus."

He bristled at my rebuke and glanced around to see if anyone else might have noticed his behaviour.

"Did she—you know, the dark one—did she see me too?"

I wanted to tell him he was of no consequence to Lilith. But to keep the fear of her powers alive in Zeus and make him heed our watchful eyes, I said nothing. After instructing Hera to summon me if required, I took myself as far away from the orgiastic revelry as I could, back to the Otherworld. I needed to ready myself for the events that were about to unfold.

Hephaistos had completed the throne designed to entrap Zeus. Now he only waited for the moment to unveil it. He and the Cyclopes polished it day and night until it gleamed bright yellow-gold, an irresistible enticement fit to flatter Zeus. Under Hera's instruction, invisible fetters had been placed upon the throne to restrain whoever sat upon it. The day of the union would be the perfect occasion to present the ingenious gift to her husband.

"I dearly regret not speaking with you and Lilith about my decision to summon Aphrodite here," she said to me. "It was a terrible mistake. Can you not enchant her away somewhere? In that guise, she is as self-serving as Zeus. I want her gone."

Much as it pained me on behalf of Hera and Hephaistos, I knew Aphrodite was simply playing her role. Her unassailable beauty and seductive charms were contrived as weapons. For femina, her presence was divisive. She was either disdained for her self-absorbed ways or exalted and slavishly emulated, inspiring femina to seek the male gaze of approval as she did or get in sparring contests with each other like male-kind. It amused us Ancients that Aphrodite herself had jealous serpent eyes, though she had little compassion for it in others.

The day of the union brought matters to a head for Hera. None of us knew how Hephaistos had discovered his mother's disdain for Aphrodite. But I suspected the ubiquitous Hermes was at the centre of it. Hephaistos had secretly swapped the thrones of Hera and Zeus to ensure it would be Hera who was rendered immobile so as not to prevent his union with his new bride. When she sat upon the throne, the fetters locked into place on her wrists. Hera threw back her head and laughed, pretending to be complicit with the deed, as if it were a nod to her reluctance to remarry Zeus. But in truth she had been deeply shocked by her son's stinging treachery.

"Pour as much ambrosia as you can for the guests," I instructed Dionysus, the oenophile of the pantheon.

"Use whatever potion necessary to blur their memory, especially Hera's. But none for Hephaistos. Find him a key to loosen the fetters on that throne as soon as you can."

Always comfortable amid drama, Dionysus did as he was instructed. Before long, a repentant Hephaistos stood in front of his mother, ready to unlock the throne.

"Dearest mother, please forgive me," he mumbled in tears.

Silenced by her wounded pride, she convulsed with pain when she stepped out of the chair. Oblivious to her misery, Zeus grabbed Hera by the waist and twirled her around the great hall, dancing until she tore herself away from him, exhausted. Her sisters came to her rescue, whisking her away from the melee and out of sight. Hestia wrapped her arms around Hera, who sobbed on her shoulder in self-pity and defeat.

Demeter could not stop herself from ranting. "I blame Zeus and all male-kind like him for this," she said. "He has shown them that the femina can be treated however they wish."

"Why did you sanction my reunion with him?" Hera said to me, as tears merged with spittle at the corner of her mouth.

She and her sisters glared at me with hostile, questioning faces. Lilith appeared in front of us with her usual impeccable timing.

"Do not blame Hekate or any of the femina for the rise of the power of the gods," she said without a trace of emotion. "The worst that can be done is that we turn upon each other. The simple truth is that Hephaistos believes himself in love with Aphrodite. Even a mother's love cannot override such a powerful seduction."

"Then why did you not intervene?" Hera cried.

"It was you who summoned her, Hera. Aphrodite has merely loosened the bond between a mother and a son. It is as it is meant to be," Lilith said.

"Why then will you not control the pantheon, take control over the gods and their behaviour toward the femina?" Hera asked us.

"We cannot enter portals that have been closed to us," Lilith explained. "The gods see us as messengers from the primordial Darkness, as heralds of their Death. They will not even dare to look toward the Light within the Darkness, let alone surrender to it. Their greatest fear is that it will diminish the power they hold. Thus, they will continue to disavow us."

Athena and Artemis, the new wave of femina guardians, had been standing in the wings as Hestia and Demeter pulled Hera to her feet.

"Then I shall remain a maiden and fight them on their own ground," Athena announced. "I shall show male-kind and femina my strategy *and* artistry. No one shall make me a bride or conquer me. That is my pledge."

"And mine," echoed Artemis. "I will show them how to be both hunter *and* nurturer. And I shall name my seven hounds after each of the seven sisters of the Cosmos, the Pleiades. The gods will squirm on their thrones when my Sacred Bitches rise to my call."

"As you wish," Lilith said. We all made the sign of the dove on our foreheads. "With your Aegis and your Sacred

Owl, Athena, you and your artful skills shall forever be revered. With your Sacred Bitches and your night wisdom, Artemis, you shall be revered alongside the Pleiades as you light the night sky as the Great She-Bear, protector of the Tree of Life in the Heavens."

Lilith had bestowed powerful gifts on the two young Goddesses. Artemis held her crescent-shaped silver bow above her head, gleaming like a nimbus Moon of old. Athena lifted her beloved shield, the Aegis, high in the air, the sign of victory in battle.

"Hekate and I must remain as we are until the darkness in them becomes intolerable and we are called upon again," Lilith continued. "It is as it is." A swirl of vapour, and Lilith was gone again.

Demeter sighed loudly and said, "She doesn't understand that in the meantime the memory of us may be lost forever."

A voice came back to her from the aethers.

"We shall never be fully forgotten, Demeter. On that you can rely."

Delighted by their new status, Artemis and Athena raised a cheer with youthful zeal. Hera had regained her composure, though her Light was still dimmed by the ordeal. That Hephaistos had sought Aphrodite's approval over her own had marked yet another change in the pantheon. The bitter taste of jealousy had arisen among us. It felt like a stony wall obstructing the path to Heart-Soul. If I had not already an inkling about other concerns for Demeter, I might have suspected that she herself felt a prick of jealousy for her daughter's sake as she watched

Athena and Artemis. She had great hopes for darling Persephone, seeking a status for her as high as that of the other young Goddesses.

Looking back, I wonder that I didn't act on my fleeting premonitions about Demeter. But my faith in my own Knowing had become more diminished than I cared to admit. Only the strongest of summons could now call me into vision. And that was about to happen.

Demeter

Goddess of the Harvest ~
Keeper of the Eleusinian Rites

Poor dear Demeter. The disappearance of a child is a mother's worst nightmare, and Demeter was the most anxious, protective mother in all of Olympos. When the news came that Persephone had vanished while deep in the woods planting narcissus, she quickly summoned me.

"She has never done this before, simply disappeared!" she said. "Those witless Dryads left her on her own. No femina is safe anymore, especially if they are newly blossoming. I don't know how many times I have told her to be vigilant."

She heaved with sobs, crying into her horse's mane as he nestled his head on her shoulder. Arion's coat glistened with sweat. Demeter had ridden him hard, searching frantically for Persephone. The horse's loyal eyes begged me to help her.

"We will find her, Demeter," I said determinedly, as shaken by the event as she.

"You must ask that monstrous brother of mine where she is. I cannot bear to see him lie to my face," she spat. "But he would not dare lie to you. And I promise you this, if he is responsible, I will find a way to make him suffer if it is the last thing I do."

When I descended in front of Zeus, he was dozing noisily on his throne. He awoke with a start and looked at me with panic, relieved to see Lilith was not there, too.

"My dearest beauty, have you come to pleasure me like in the old days?" he said.

The flares of my torches burst into flames such was my rage at the remark. He gripped the arms of his throne in fright.

"What is it?" he said. "I have been faultless in my conduct."

"It is a matter of the utmost urgency I bring you," I said. "Persephone has vanished. Demeter is distraught beyond all reason. What do you know of this?"

He lunged out of his throne with a thunderous boom, sending his retinue of acolytes scurrying away like mice.

"Who has taken sweet Persephone?!" He bellowed, loud enough to resound over all of Olympos.

"Who knows anything of this?" he bellowed again.

As he spoke, I saw the tiniest speck of light far, far away, too fleeting to grasp, like a point at the edge of a star. Someone knew something.

"Tell Demeter I will search for her darling daughter in every corner of Olympos," he said.

"I hardly need tell you that if you had anything to do with this and Lilith hears of it—"

"Not I," he said, shaking his woolly tangle of hair.

He set off purposefully, his countless minions following him like twittering sparrows. I decided to leave him to his search while I went to look beyond the realms, fearing she may be lost to another existence.

Meanwhile, Demeter searched the aethers day and night. Her plaintive cries seeped into every crevice of the sombre silence on Olympos. The pantheon grieved along with her, fearing the worst. As she travelled onward to faraway Eleusis in search of Persephone, Demeter paused in her lament. I was surprised to hear laughter. Had Persephone returned to her? I rushed to Demeter's side, but there, instead, was Baubo. The Ancient Goddess of Mirth Wisdom had appeared to Demeter in Eleusis to cheer and strengthen her. She was a femina trickster who revelled in bawdy ribaldry. She was known to lift her robes to show her pudenda and shake her naked breasts while dancing. Baubo had taken Demeter by surprise, inspiring a belly laugh.

"Have you seen my Persephone?" she asked Baubo.

I had never known Baubo to be mournful, but Demeter's grief moved her to cease prancing. She grimaced and shook her head no.

"I see through the eyes of my nipples that Persephone has a destiny of her own. You must honour this," she said, before disappearing.

While searching for her daughter, Demeter had abandoned her role as Goddess of the Harvest and abundance in the Cosmos. She punished us all with her ceaseless grieving, creating a winter with no end. Her icy tears froze the earth and chilled the mortals' bones to the marrow.

"This is hard on the mortals," I told her. "Every living thing is suffering."

She looked at me with vacant eyes, not grasping my words. Her dishevelled robes and matted locks reeked.

"They do not know *my* suffering," she said.

"The mortals have had nothing to do with Persephone's disappearance," I said, reaching into her thoughts. "Helios cannot do his work of bringing the warmth of the sun to the Earth every day."

No sooner had I bid Demeter farewell than I felt it— the Knowing of who I needed to seek for the Truth. Helios! The speck of light I had seen at Persephone's disappearance was now like a distant arrow of sunlight, a ray of solar dust.

I approached Helios as he was finishing his daily ride over the gloomy grey Heavens. Six Moon cycles of darkened misery had now passed.

"Oh, Hekate, it is you! You startled me, sneaking up like that."

Flames streaked from the nostrils of his golden stallions as he pulled at their reins and halted the gilded chariot. It was ornately carved with whorls on the rim like the curling tresses of the Oceanids. It was one of Hephaistos's finest works.

"So, what's been happening down there on Olympos? Who's been raising havoc with the seasons? My labours seem pointless in this endless mist and fog."

"Helios, what do you know of Persephone's disappearance? Answer me truthfully. What did you see?"

He shifted around on his plush gold-covered seat.

"I don't want to bring attention to myself over this," he said. "Apollo made it hard enough for me to get this job, I don't want to have it snatched away."

I could have slapped him. Twice. He had ridden to and fro, every single day, knowing that all hell had broken loose in the Heavens, and yet he had said and done nothing. As I held the shadowy Truth mirror before him, he put up his hands to shield him from the solipsist he had become.

Lilith suddenly appeared, scowling with anger. With a snap of her fingers, she turned the fading light of day into deepest night.

"Speak, Helios!" she commanded. "Fear not, there will be no repercussions. You are already enslaved to an endless task. Why do you think young Apollo passed it on to you?"

While sailing across the skies in his golden chariot every day, feeling as grand as an old Titan god, he had failed his duty to be Watcher over the Heavens during the light of day, and he knew it.

"I was waiting for one of you to tell me what had happened," he mumbled feebly.

"The passage of the Moon as the Eternal Light in the Darkness is ours to watch over," I said. "The journey of the Sun each day is yours to oversee. You saw fit to tell Hephaistos about Aphrodite being unfaithful with Ares. Yet, you could not bring yourself to tell Demeter about seeing her daughter vanish?"

He covered his face in humiliation, hiding from the Light of the crescent Moon as it slowly ascended.

"It all happened so quickly, I could scarcely believe my eyes. One moment, Persephone was planting flowers, as pretty as a picture, surrounded by butterflies; the next moment, I saw her slipping through a crevice in the Earth."

"Hades," Lilith said to me in the silence. "Budding femina swallowed again by the devouring male-kind."

Helios's stallions became agitated, lifting their hind quarters and kicking his chariot; the flames from their nostrils lit the night sky with green and crimson fire. They had come from the same stock as Demeter's mare.

Helios tried to soothe the horses. Then he said, "I know I have made an unforgiveable mistake by saying nothing. I turned a blind eye hoping someone else would come forward."

"You made yourself complicit in the deed. This is what male-kind has become," I said. "Unseeing and complicit like you. It is a very grave error of judgement you have made. And one you must now live with."

Helios slunk away in shame; his stallions stood beside the chariot in protest, refusing to budge, forcing him to go on alone. Lilith and I set out to find Zeus and question him again.

When Zeus saw us coming toward his throne, he shook with fear. The acolytes at his side screamed and stampeded from the throne room, fighting to get through the door. Lilith's gigantic silhouette in my torch light was indeed a terrifying sight, even to me.

"You knew!" I said, as we approached him.

"He only told me of it after you had been to visit me," he pleaded. "I begged him to release her, but he wouldn't listen."

"Yes," I hissed at him. "I'll bet Hades said if it's fair game for you to take femina for yourself, it's fair game for him, too. You are an utter disgrace."

"He said he had fallen in love with Persephone. He begged me for her hand. I knew Demeter would not hear of it. She had already turned down Apollo's and Hermes's offers."

"Persephone's future was not yours to decide, Zeus," Lilith said, sighing. "And may I remind you, you are all merely one-existence gods. I told you to make good of the time that remains. There have been too many others like you. We watch you come and then, finally, you all go again."

He flinched at the words, shrivelling like a sea sponge on hot sand. Zeus knew his time was all but over.

"And if you warn Hades that Hekate is about to visit him, the Erinyes, the Empousai and the Moirai will see to your immediate destruction," she added. "The Cosmos does not require petty filial loyalties for its evolution."

Lilith had drawn the night to its stillest so that her declaration could be heard by all. I could not resist smiling to myself at her virtuosity. The mere mention of the Erinyes, nicknamed the Furies, was enough to send shudders rippling through anyone's bones. They were the Goddesses of vengeance and retribution, and even more indifferent to the cycles of existence than Lilith, whom they adored. Tisiphone took care of retaliation and destruction duties. Megaera took care of grudges against the person. And Alecto did all the unspeakable things that no one wanted to consider.

The Moirai, the Fates, were gentler in their expression but no less exacting. Clotho was happy to spin and weave the threads of each existence, and Lachesis to measure the worthiness of the weave. But Atropos would happily cut the woven threads if an existence no longer served its purpose.

The two Empousai, Lamia, and Mormolykeia, were still young in the Cosmos. They were being taught by Lilith to be her assistants. The half-serpent, half-femina seductresses, who could fly and swim like ancient daimons, were already feared. They terrorized those who ran amok, oblivious to others.

"That Soul-less misbegotten creature," Demeter ranted. "He has gone entirely mad in that infernal realm he governs. Hades and Zeus are true sons of Kronos. They are as depraved and loathsome as he. And to take the purest femina of all, my darling Persephone, down to that hellhole. I will never forgive him."

For all the courage that urged her forward, Demeter paled and hesitated as we approached Thanatos, the surly-looking, lumpish giant at the forbidding doors to the Underworld. He was a son of Nyx, the Goddess of Night and Chaos. As a very young Goddess, I had often spent time with him and his siblings, Morpheus and Hypnos, before Lilith took me under her wing. Demeter stood back in shock as he silently embraced me and stepped aside for us to enter the door.

The journey to the Underworld could only be undertaken by someone like me, someone who did not fear Death in its many guises. Demeter clung to my arm as my torches flared, lighting up the horrors in the murky swamp. The entrance was surrounded by corpses, flyblown and putrid, with maggots and vermin feasting on the rotting flesh. A gigantic elm stood by the door, looking monstrous in the shadows with its thickened knots and gnarled roots. Demeter jumped in fright as a rotten limb fell to the ground with a thud.

Three Judges seated inside the doors studied us with hostile curiosity. They had been mortals, but upon their death, Zeus had appointed them to the position of overlords, as they had lionised him. We ignored their arrogant posturing. One of them had the temerity to call out and ask us to explain ourselves as we passed by. I tipped a flaming torch toward him and burned his raggedy garments to cinders. The Erinyes standing to the left of them laughed like hyenas. Charon was lounging in his boat, waiting to be called to ferry new arrivals across the river to meet their fate in the Underworld.

"What brings you here, Hekate? Come for a holiday? Brought a friend for company, have you?"

"A comedian now as well as a ferryman, Charon?" I said. The Erinyes howled with laughter again.

Demeter suddenly caught her breath. In our haste to reach Persephone, I had forgotten to warn her about the grotesque inhabitants of the Underworld. The Harpies, the Gorgons, Chimera and Hydra, and every other creature of Death, had emerged from the darkness to see what the commotion was about. Each one appearing in the procession before us was more hideous than the last; the

Souls of the creatures were as poisonous as black mamba venom.

"Hold tight, dear one," I whispered. "Their plight was borne from the absence of Love in their Souls. Until they embrace the Light of Truth within them, they will never know Death in its glorious fullness. This is to be their lot."

Cerberus, frothing from all three mouths, snarled and barked at us in the shadows. When he saw my torches, he came and nuzzled at me, basking in my attention as I patted his heads.

Moving forth, past the Fields of Punishment, I covered Demeter's eyes to spare her the sight of the horrors there. It was the place of reckoning for the sickest of mortal Souls. Beyond it we came to the Asphodel meadows, where unfulfilled Souls roamed aimlessly through the tall yellow and pink-white flowers. The Mourning Fields nearby were crowded with the pitiable Souls who had wasted their lives in pursuit of unrequited love. My torches offered them hope for redemption, and as I passed by, I released their suffering, enabling them to enter the Elysion Fields for succour and forgiveness.

The Isles looming ahead, outside Hades's domain, had portals that only Lilith and I presided over. Wanting to strengthen Demeter's hope and faith as we ventured into the infernal depths, I pointed to the faraway Isle of the Blest.

"The Isle is the place of completion, the home of the Soul guides and teachers," I said. "It is where existences are lived in Enlightenment. Hades would have to consult with us to access the Isle. Since he's not done so, we know he has not taken Persephone there."

"It might have been better for her if he had, instead of bringing her to this hellhole," Demeter said, overwhelmed and in tears.

We trudged forward, descending further and further into the abyss of Tartarus to the dungeon where I was sure Hades had hidden the darling girl. At last, I saw a gleam of light ahead, coming toward us. The shimmer of gold was unmistakeable. It was the Caduceus, the golden wand that never left Hermes's side.

"I should have known you would be part of this, Hermes," I said.

Hermes had followed me to the Underworld early in his existence, his curiosity overriding any fears he may have had. Since then, he had navigated its labyrinth of passages many times himself, casting his own special charm over everyone. He had no qualms about playing the fool with the hostile Underworld inhabitants. Lilith was the only one in the Cosmos to whom he was truly deferential. Otherwise, he was simply a law unto himself, going wherever he wanted to go, seeing whomever he wanted to see, and doing whatever he liked.

"Dearest, loveliest, Hekate. Oh, and Demeter, too, I see," he said, as he drew closer.

Demeter grabbed his ear and took his prized wand from him.

"Ouch! Do you mind, Demeter? Give me back my wand!"

She twisted his earlobe so hard he almost fell backward.

"Take me to my daughter now!" she hissed at him, whacking him hard on his pert little bottom with his own wand.

"You are in a foul mood, I must say."

"TAKE ME TO HER NOW!!" she shouted in his face.

He turned around to march back in the direction from which he had come. My torches illumined a blackened oak door hidden at the end of the tunnel, and we hastened toward it. Hermes lifted the great iron bar from the door and threw it open. There, inside, was Persephone. She was sitting with Hades at a grand table in the middle of what once had been a dungeon. I was relieved to see her looking as lively and lovely as ever, and that she had been housed in luxurious quarters. The room was lined with silks and brocades, and perfumed with candles in every niche—a room fit for a queen. She turned to us in joy and disbelief.

"Mother!"

Demeter swept her child into her arms and smothered her pretty auburn hair with kisses. Hermes used the distraction to grab his wand from Demeter, protecting his swollen ear with the other hand. Hades, who was hunched over the table, had the pinched look of the guilty. Hermes sat down on a stool beside him, away from Demeter and me. His eyes danced around us, excited by the prospect of witnessing what was about to unfold.

"Aunty Hekate," Persephone said, hugging me tight. "Thank you with all my heart for coming to find me. Though it hasn't been as bad here as I feared it might.

Hades has looked after me very well, in fact," she added, nodding in his direction.

As Hades was shuffling onto his feet, Demeter walked over to him and whacked his old, grey-bearded face hard with the back of her hand. It was considered the greatest of insults to do so, denoting an utter lack of regard.

"You've made her eat something, haven't you? To trick her into staying here? I thought brother Zeus was the lowest of the gods, but it turns out that it is you."

Persephone intervened.

"Mother, please. I know you are angry. I have something to say that may help to make sense of the whole situation."

Persephone took Demeter's hand and led her to a seat at the other end of the table, sitting down beside her.

"I have been biding my time until one of you came here to witness my Knowing."

Her calm countenance was a surprise to all of us— Hades, especially, who looked at Persephone as if he had never seen her before.

"Well," she began. "Once I got over the shock of being stolen away to this place, I began looking deep into my Knowing as I observed everything here," she said, looking at Hermes.

"When you sought my hand in marriage not long ago, Hermes, you were so charming. But here you have been nothing but a fool, chattering on like a monkey, thinking me too innocent and stupid to know what was afoot. But I have been a step ahead of you both," she said, looking over at Hades.

She got up from the table and sedately paced across the room. She could not have appeared more regal had she been wearing a crown and carrying a staff.

"I knew exactly what you were about when you offered me the pomegranate seeds, Hades. I heard this monkey proposing the plan to you," she said, patting Hermes on the head as she walked past him.

Demeter glared at Hermes and pushed her chair away from the table, as if she intended to go over and backhand his face as well. He covered his ear and held his wand in front of him like a sword.

"You deserve worse than a twisted ear, Hermes," she said. "I will deal with you later."

I came and stood alongside Demeter to present a united front. I felt a cold gush of air and knew that Lilith had arrived and stealthily watched us.

"Carry on, my darling, tell us what you have witnessed," Demeter said to the glowing Persephone.

"I am sorry, Mother, you may not like what I have decided to do, but I believe I have used sound judgement. Hermes suggested that Hades tell me a story, to say he regretted bringing me here, and then offer me fancy food and wine as a token of his esteem while we waited for you to arrive."

"Hermes overheard you talking with Zeus, Aunty. He is quite the eavesdropper."

Lilith whipped an invisible whirlwind around Hermes, making him fall off his stool. We laughed without kindness.

"So, I decided to play along with their game," Persephone continued. "Hades became more and more desperate to make me eat something. And Hermes tried to cajole me, too, with all his clever talk, as if I did not know that by doing so, I would be locked down here for Eternity. Hades polished a ripened pomegranate and cut it in half, knowing it to be my favourite treat. Then he delicately pulled out the seeds, saying he would feed them to me, one by one."

She smiled to herself. "I allowed him to feed me six, and only six. I had decided—and I am sorry, Mother, but I think once you hear me out, you will agree. I decided to be joined with Hades, and I shall stay here for six Moon cycles. They will be the seasons of autumn and winter, to keep the Hearth warm and the Altar lit as Aunty Hestia has taught me, and to govern with fairness like Aunty Hera has shown me. I shall return to Olympos for the spring and summer seasons, Mother, to help with the harvest. And to help you at Eleusis. Just think of the Death knowledge I will bring to the Mysteries!"

"But, why?!" Demeter protested.

Persephone raised her hand.

"Please, let me finish."

Demeter nodded and held her tongue.

"The Underworld needs a Goddess. It weighs too heavily toward male-kind. It is an intolerable place as you will have seen, Mother. It has become the wasteland Great-Aunt Lilith said it would be when male-kind claimed ownership and we Goddesses were banished from its depths."

She turned her attention to me.

"I now can see why your Lampades retreated in exile, Aunty Hekate. I would like them to return again."

The mere mention of my wonderful Lampades brought a sob of grief to my throat. How I had missed them. The nocturnal, torch-bearing nymphs of the Underworld rivers had been gifted to me by Nyx in my early times as a Goddess. The ten of them had fled to the Great Darkness when the Underworld became overwhelmed by male-kind.

"If you and Aunty Hekate agree to help me, and Great-Aunt Lilith, too, we can restore the Transition between endings and beginnings. We will make Death the Great Mystery and celebration it always was once again. You have trained me in this Wisdom, all of you. I know it is my destiny. And I can put up with him," she said, sweeping her hand toward Hades. "He has simply played his part."

Demeter reached for my arm to steady herself. I felt the corners of my mouth twitching, as it always did when hearing words of Truth. My brilliant Goddess-daughter had done more than outwit Hades and Hermes at their own game. She had triumphed over them.

"Dear Persephone, it is you that will return the Sacred glory of Ancient Femina to the Underworld," I said. "I see now that has been your destiny all along. It was always meant to be under your care."

The glance I cast at Hades made him shiver. He had preferred to forget that the Ancient rituals of the Sacred Earth Womb, of Death and the Underworld, belonged to us.

"We must invoke the Mysteries at Eleusis to bring knowledge to the mortals of the still, small point of Creation, the Lemniscate. That way they can find the Truth and the Light within their Souls before their mortal bodies age and die," Persephone added.

Demeter and I nodded, awed by her daughter's prescience.

"It is just as Baubo foresaw," Demeter muttered under her breath. "But can she really put up with the old dolt?"

"She is kindness itself, Demeter. I would not have wished him upon her," I whispered back.

"Remember, Hades has brought about the fulfilment of this destiny, albeit unknowingly. He will step aside for her greater Knowing and Wisdom," Lilith assured silently.

Hades had sat quietly through the discourse. I could see he was impressed by his prospective wife yet disturbed by her capacity to outmanoeuvre him. And no doubt wary of her deep-rooted devotion to the Sacred Divine Femina.

"I know you're here, Lilith," he said.

Realising it was Lilith who had knocked him from his stool, Hermes scuttled under the table like a crab into a cave. She materialised as an ebony Being in front of Hades, the epitome of the Ancient Black Goddess from the beginning of time. Persephone ran over to hug her, just as she had always done. She was the only immortal on the whole of Olympos to ever do so.

"Great-Aunt Lilith! It's been so long since I have seen you!"

Lilith had made herself visible in her most Ancient form as a declaration to Hades and Hermes not only of her strong alignment with Persephone but also to show her primacy in all the Realms. Lilith and I may have been disregarded among the gods of the Hellenes, but they could not sever the powerful bonds of the Goddesses with the Divine Femina. The allegiance of the Goddesses with her and with us was Eternal.

"I expect you have something to say, Lilith," Hades said. "And Hekate," he added, nodding toward me.

We both smiled and said nothing. Enough had been made apparent. The hush and tranquillity in his underground cave felt much like being under Earth's oceans or like my home in the Otherworld. I could understand how Persephone had found peace here. She would transform the arid, hostile place the Underworld had become into a place of glorious ascension. The cyclical Transformation of Death and Rebirth would finally be restored to wise Goddess hands, as it had been in Ancient Shambhala and Lemuria, and in all of the ancestral lineages of the past.

After making a binding contract between Hades and Persephone, we took her away with us. Demeter kept her daughter close as Lilith and I led the way out of the infernal realm along the labyrinthine passageways. The sulking Hermes trailed behind us. I had heard Hades mutter "witches" under his breath as we left.

"We have been called a witch, hag, or crone so many times, Lilith," I said. "Let us claim these names for ourselves. Witch especially! The word holds the power to scare male-kind."

Our laughter bounced off the cavernous walls.

"What are you laughing at?" Demeter asked.

"We have decided we like to be called the name witch," I said.

"The name is perfect," Persephone added. "I think of the witch hazel tree that heals. It goes underground in winter and returns in the spring, and its roots are strong in the Earth, while its boughs reach to the Heavens. It is a tree of Transformation."

"Hmmph," Hermes grunted, appearing behind us in the dark passage. "Dark Moon witches, you mean."

"I like the sound of that," Demeter said. "Dark Moon Witches. It has the right ring for the Midwives of the Heavens."

That moment set our fates. Lilith had been known as Dark Moon Lilith long before the existence of the Hellenes. But my legend was more nebulous, harder to define. As I prepared to leave the pantheon and journey to the Celtic Realm, I decided to reclaim the word "Witch" and make her dance with the Moon, the Sun, and all the shadows in between. I decided to make the word my own.

Securing Persephone's place in the Underworld was our final gesture toward the salvation of femina in the pantheon. When the reign of the Hellenes came to an end, Roman rulers would rise to power and quickly replace their beliefs. As Roman legions marched on cobbled roads conquering new worlds, their new Roman gods went with them. Zeus was renamed Jupiter, Hera became Juno, and Demeter was Ceres. The orbs of the skies were given Roman names, too, so that their dominion over Earth and Heaven would be complete.

It was during Roman times that Christianity sprang from the loins of the ancient Hebrew faith of Judaism. Lilith and I tentatively welcomed the reemergence of the Light of Truth in the stories the Christians told.

The one-God of the Hebrew tales, Jehovah the Almighty, was made in the likeness of the male-kind who scribed the tales. Their God was a wrathful, unyielding, all-powerful Being who favoured suffering over Transformation, final death over renewal. The Goddess cycles of Life, Death, and Renewal were deemed to be pagan sacrifices, and thus the Sacred rituals were overridden and outlawed in the new faith. The Sacred Union of Dark and Light was severed into a warring pair of opposites—good versus evil, right versus wrong, black versus white, femina versus male-kind—separating mortals from the very fibre of their Being.

"Now we Dark Goddesses are condemned as she-devils by the Roman conquerors and the upholders of their faith," I bemoaned to Lilith. "Only the shamans of the Earth, the Seers and Knowers, still look to us for solace and Wisdom."

She shrugged, amused by our exile to the realm the Romans called the Mysterium Tremendum, the place of terrible mystery. All femina, and Nature herself, were condemned as Dark Goddess forces beyond the control of conquering male-kind. True Mystery had been replaced by dogma and the enigma of Transformation had been forsaken. The Truth of the deepest self, the essence of the Infinite Light, was forsaken along with it.

"We must help them to align with the Moon again," Lilith said. "If the mortals who worship a male-kind god remember the mystery of the Moon, they may yet find the pulse of Light within themselves and feel the thrum of the Earth."

I did not care to remind her that mortals of great Wisdom had been following the thrums of the Earth, Sun, and Moon long before the one-god came to be. There were mortals who watched the orbs in the sky for signs, listened to the whisperings of the Earth, and knew the Souls of living creatures. Their stories of the Cosmos and the Infinite Light were still fluent within them.

"I am aware of the ones who walk in the Mystery, Hekate. It is not of them I speak."

I was startled by her words. So distracted by our plight and pained by our waning existence, I had forgotten that she still could hear my every word.

"If you don't hear me speak in your thoughts, it is not that I do not hear you," she added, laughing like a wild bird as she flew into the aethers.

I had missed seeing her as often as I once had. More and more, she faded into the far reaches of the penumbra. Even on the brightest of whole Moon nights, when the radiant orb mirrored herself in the many waters of the Earth, she had seemed faint and distant. She had seemed all but lost to me.

"Hekate," she said out of the darkness. "I have always been here. It is you who have been lost."

The sheer truth of it sliced through me like a xiphos (the ancients' double-edged sword). No matter the shape or form, Lilith was always watchful and prescient, the constant to my inconstancy. Indeed, it was I who had gotten lost, as I struggled to accept the changes being wrought.

"Think of Khairon," Lilith added, from the depths of darkness. "It was you who taught him how to be a Wounded Healer, to be an exemplar for those who suffered in the pantheon. It is time to remember your own teachings."

Khairon, half-brother to Zeus, was a noble Centaur who bridged the divide between the low instincts and the higher Knowing, as I had shown him. With his kindness and compassion, he had chosen to live beyond the despoliation on Olympos. As his gentle Being came into my vision, I was indeed reminded of my very own teachings, forgotten in the midst of pain.

For a time, after the demise of the pantheon, I had become immersed in a Death cycle as black as the nigredo. Carrying the suffering Soul of the Divine Femina had pierced my immortal heart. All sense of my Being had been lost to me. Deeply wounded once again, this time by the loss of the Dark Goddess myth, I had disappeared along with it into the wordless place, dying unto myself. Invisible. I had forgotten that these long, lonely black descents were but two of a thousand deaths before the final Death.

I had forgotten, as well, the purpose of the Darkness. That it was created for the rising of a new dawn, a Transformation epitomized by the Balsamic Moon cycle. A vision of the Divine Serpent, the Ouroboros, had appeared before me; the circular tail-biting motif reminded me that I had been shedding a skin, seeking a change in my aloneness, harmonising the new learning with the old. Until that moment, I had not recognised my journey as one of Ancient Alchemy. Glimmers of the Light of Rebirth and Renewal now beckoned. It was time for me to undergo another cycle of existence.

"Stay close by, Lilith," I said. "I am going to descend closer to the world of the mortals and I will need you there to assist. My work requires more than visits to their Seeings, Knowings, and Dreams. I want to be there alongside them in the earthly realm."

"Ah," she said. "That is what I have been waiting for. You have been through the Eye of the Fire. Another cycle of your Alchemy is complete. Now your task is to help the mortals keep the wondrous Moon in their visions and hold fast to her Wisdom."

"It is time for Dark Moon Witchery!" I laughed, naively believing a smoother path lay ahead.

"They need no longer fear Death and our Dark Moon, Hekate. Guide them to the glorious labyrinth within them. To the Light!"

"To the Light!" I said, so giddy with excitement I failed to hear Lilith's parting words:

"Hold fast to all you have learned. The cycles end only to begin again. There are always new perils to face on each journey."

PART THREE

The Celtic Realm

Celtic Earth

After farewelling Lilith, I descended to dwell in the breathtaking splendour of the indigo Earth. To be in its sphere was to have every bit of me awakened, as if shimmering with starlight. I journeyed to the far reaches of the Earth, where the diamond-white crystals dazzled me and the arctic air crept tingling into every pore. I revelled in the salty brine of Earth's clear blue oceans, feeling cleansed and invigorated as I dived and swam in its thriving waters. I flew over vast deserts of rock and sand, mesmerized by the blazing sun. I walked in forests thick with trees in glorious colours. Braiding rivers sang their way across the land with their sweet music, and the waters from secret springs and waterfalls slaked my thirst. I found myself enraptured at every moment.

Word of my descent to Earth's portals had spread like whirling dandelion seeds. That I was not as forgotten in the Earthly sphere as I had thought was encouraging to me. Soon I was summoned to a gathering on the Isle of Avalon by the Druidic Council and The Many. It was to be held on the night of the rising crescent Moon; the one they named the Horned Moon.

They assembled in the Grove of the Willows, waiting for me in that Sacred place on the mystical Isle found only by the Knowers. As I emerged in their presence with the rising Moon, I saw the gods and goddesses of many different peoples congregated there, the ones they called The Many. The meeting looked to be urgent, more than a simple welcome. The conqueror ways of male-kind in the Hellenes had skewed my Seeing, for I expected the first to step forward would be Myrddin the Diviner, or the Dagda, the gigantic All Father of the Tuatha De Danaan. But these were the Druids, or Draiochta, as they called themselves. Here in their realm, male-kind and femina lived together as equals, not separated by role, nor by shape nor form. Like Lilith and me, they spoke without saying words aloud—an art from our shared Atlantean past.

"Greetings, Hekate," said Medbh, the protector of the Draiochta in the Grove, in her silent tongue as she stepped forward to embrace me. "We, Draiochta and Knowers, humbly welcome you here among us."

Medbh was the Goddess of Battle and the Goddess of Sacred Marriage, the Hieros Gamos of her people. It was like having the spirits of Hera and Aphrodite with me again. The very air around the Draiochta was like a sigh of calmness. At last, I was in a realm where I was among Kindred Souls. It was as if I had come home.

One by one, they came to embrace me, quietly whispering their names in the silent night. I sensed my way into the essence of each of them, feeling their warm breaths do the same with me. They sat down around me on oak-tree stumps carved with a triple spiral—the Doire Knot of Eternity, their symbol for Life, Death, and Rebirth.

"It is an honour to be with you all," I said, pivoting around the circle with my hands on my forehead in the sign of the Goddess. "I can see you truly are The Many on this occasion, which tells me there are concerns among you and your people."

Cyrridwen tossed her long black windswept hair and invited me to sit between her and Carnonos in the circle. Cyrridwen, Goddess of the Grain, was known for the healing potions made in her cauldron. Like Demeter, she was fiercely watchful over her beautiful daughter.

Carnonos, beside me, wore antlers strapped to his head in honour of the beasts of the forest. His oaken harp was slung over his back, its strings untouched and cold in these troubled times. Sacred animals surrounded us. Owls, crows, and ravens perched in the willow trees, watching us with hooded eyes. Black dogs and cats lay at our feet, while wolves the size of bears prowled around the circle. Restless horses shuffled their hooves in the dust as the wolves passed by.

Sitting opposite me in the circle was Morrigan the Mother with her consort, the Dagda. She was their femina shape-shifter, taking the faces of Anu the Maiden and Badb the Crone as required, a triple Goddess in herself.

Rhiannon, sitting to the left of Morrigan, shone like the moon at perigee. She was their Moon Goddess, the ruler of the Otherworld and the Spirit of Dreams. I had heard her called Queen of the Faeries by the mortals. Some said they saw her flitting through the leafy boughs in the woods or out riding her chestnut red horse, her flame-red hair flying in the wind.

Morrigan in her role as Badb the Crone, the Elder, stood to command the gathering.

"Hekate, welcome to the Earthly portal in which we dwell. We gather here together in the Sacred Grove to seek your and Lilith's Wisdom and guidance at this time."

I had already divined what they wished to speak about. I hoped that Lilith was close by.

"We are being driven into the shadows like deamhans, denigrated as evil and denied by the talkers of this new god sweeping through our lands," Morrigan said. She spoke this aloud, as the silent words were not strong enough to carry the weight of her despair.

Myrddin removed his tapered hat and ruffled his hair as Morrigan passed him the talking wand to speak. Myrddin was the eldest of the Draiochta, an Ancient shaman and Seer. The wand was as tall as he and ornately wrought like Hephaistos's work. The Doire-knot ironwork at the top of it glowed with the Eternal Flame in its centre. It was his masterpiece, made with the help of the craftsman, Lugh.

"These talkers tell our people that our stories and prophesies are nonsense," he said, running his hand down the length of his ancient white beard. "They say I am nothing but an evil sorcerer. The talkers are blind to their own sorcery, telling the people of a fearsome and punishing god, and that their only salvation is to repent. The people tremble and cower with fear."

Morrigan took the wand again. "Why do the mortals believe these black-robed talkers and their stories?" she said. "What is it about them that has turned their heads? Some stories in their book speak simple truths. Yet these talkers make peril of them, twisting the words into tales of purgatory instead. I do not understand why the black robes are in Celtic lands among our mortals? Is it riches they seek?"

The wand teetered dangerously in the air as she threw up her hands in frustration, startling the sleeping cats and dogs. The ravens flapped their wings, unsettling the smaller birds perched in the branches. The wolves stopped prowling around the circle, unnerving the horses who had become used to their restless pacing. The unblinking owls remained still and watchful.

Rhiannon stood up and reached for the wand from Morrigan.

"Why are there so few femina in the stories they tell? The black-robes say their book of God has more wisdom than our ancient lore. And yet they have no Goddess to sit beside their God. Why are the mortals believing the black-robes' nonsense?"

Abnoba of Gaul made her way forward to take the wand. She had colored herself in the blue woad markings of the Picts, the Draiochta symbols painted bright and bold on her body.

"The black-robes have forbidden the mortals from worshipping in the forests and waters and giving thanks to the guardians of Nature. They tell them this Earth and the ways of the Draiochta do not matter. They say only the one-god is worthy of their reverence. This I do not understand."

Overcome by tears, Anoba handed the wand to Brigid as she rose from her seat. Brigid was their Hestia, their

Altar and Hearth Goddess, a Wisdom Keeper and Goddess of Fertility. She was their wellspring of comfort.

"With our guidance and our blessings, the mortals make homes and raise their families," she began. "They toil hard on the land, planting and harvesting with spirit knowledge from the Devic realm. But the black-robes are making them forget this Wisdom. We ache for their loss of Knowing, forgetting we are there beside them. We ache for them."

The sound of weeping could be heard at the gathering as she spoke her augury. One by one, The Many shared their observations, their bewilderment, their pain. They were already under siege. I knew only too well what it was like to be disavowed, to be cast out, beyond the reach of the mortals' grasp.

Brigid handed me the wand. I took my time before speaking, carefully choosing my words. I wanted to commune in their lilting silent tongue to ease their grieving. Lilith had descended to their portal to stand behind me; the icy burn of her presence emboldened me.

"The Great Change brings forth the new order of Being. As mortals lose their Knowing and trust in the cycles of Nature, its unpredictable ways will breed dread and terror in them. They will lose their wonder and seek to rule Nature instead of worshipping it."

I moved to stand beside Lilith.

"The black-robes tell them it is only the one-god that brings certainty—like an almighty father that will take care of them," I continued. "They say the only way they will be saved from burning in hell is by heeding and obeying their rules."

Morrigan reached for the wand.

"Are they to become like children, unable to fend for themselves? Will we become invisible to them?" she asked.

Lilith gestured to Morrigan to hand her the wand. The gathering, including every bird and animal, had been aware of her presence. All were hushed in the pure Light and Dark Void that encircled her. The talking wand glowed as Lilith began to speak.

"Draiochta, all of you here," she began. "You, like us, will never be forgotten. We must remain in the subtle realms, for a time, while we wait for the mortals to complete the sequence of learnings they will need in order to grow. For many of them, it will take many, many lifetimes. And some will remain at a standstill in these lives."

"But what will happen to the hum of the Earth while they are learning?" Abnoba of Gaul asked, the talking wand still glowing in Lilith's hand.

"It is as the omens have foretold," Morrigan said. "It is not the forces of Nature that will lay waste to the lands and waters. It is the mortals themselves."

"As it may be," Lilith said. "Fear will replace their Knowing and Wisdom. The lure of riches will distract and divide them. Greed will fester among them. Not until mortals are scourged by disease and they see the destruction of their home on Earth will a true awakening unfold."

The Many looked around the circle at one another, the voices within them stilled.

"The one-god has arisen at a time when the conquerors were already set on taming Nature and banishing the Dark Goddess. They will break the bond between the Earth and the mortals. Those in power will speak as if they hold all Knowing. Femina will be silenced. The black-robed ones will teach mortal femina to submit their will to male-kind and relinquish the power of their Wisdom. The loss of this Sacred Light will be a heavy burden for all."

A thick mist closed in around us like dense black smoke.

"How can you be sure a change will come for those in the grip of greed and malice?" Brigid as Wisdom Keeper asked on behalf of us all. "Conquerors do not cede that over which they have gained power."

"What you speak is Truth, Brigid," said Lilith. "We ourselves must hold the vision for the mortals and the wondrous orb of Earth. We must stay alongside the mortal Seers and Knowers in each of the lifetimes. It is they who will remove the masks of fear and greed and speak the unwanted Truths. It will be dangerous for them, and arduous to stay the course. They will be the unwanted ones—scapegoats, bearing the burden for speaking what most don't wish to hear."

Faint wisps of daylight seeped through the mist in the Willow Grove. With daybreak, The Many were fading from view, as were Lilith and I. The talking wand glowed softly as Lilith passed it back to Morrigan.

"Blessed be for your presence and words, Lilith and Hekate. Your Wisdom kindles Hope," Morrigan said.

Before she left, Lilith added the word of caution I had expected. Unlike me and the hapless mortals, she was not afraid of the Eye of the Fire, the descent to chaos that preceded Transformation.

"I remind you," she said, with a whip of her primordial tail, "the paths through the lifetimes to come will be arduous. The Truth-speakers will be shown no mercy. Femina will be tortured and burned. Male-kind will be driven to hide their mortal frailties and will show no mercy. Those who speak the Truth will be tortured and burned. A deep chasm of chaos between the forces of Light and the Dark will ensue. Stay the course."

After she vanished, Lilith's words hung in the air, pelting down upon us like icy stones. A lone raven's cry echoed the distress in everyone's hearts. It was left to me to soften the blow.

"Lilith calls this passage through chaos the 'Era of Divergence,'" I tried to explain. "We and the Knowers must endure the chaos to keep the recreation of the Cosmos alive. We must keep the spirit of change flowing through us like the living waters of Earth."

I wished to ask Lilith if Earth and the mortals would survive the tempests ahead. Not that she would have told me if she knew. I was already worn thin by the greed-mongers I had seen among the mortals—by their wilful blindness, their vanity, their grasping for power. They wore the gaudy trappings of success like badges pinned to their chests, without prizing the Wisdom of deep Knowing.

Morrigan restored order to the gathering, speaking words aloud to calm our distress: "Let us meet again at Bealtaine. We shall share the soma then. Bring your harp, Carnonos. You too, Lugh. Let us find joys to ease our sorrows there. We have much to do."

Before the Blood Moon gathering on the Isles at the tip of Caledonii lands, I decided to visit among the Picts and the other dwellers of the lands—the Northmen and women, the Britons, Scots, and Angles. I also took a journey around the virescent Isle of Eire. I knew the Romans feared the Eirish and the Caledonii peoples, whose woods they found impenetrable, whose languages were incomprehensible, and whose traditions baffled them.

The Roman traders who did business with the Eirish heard fantastical stories of the savagery of the Eirish people, tales of man-eating and the brutal violation of femina. It was Draiochta strategy at work to keep the Roman legions from Eirish shores. The learned, multilingual Draiochta served as intermediaries between the Eirish and the Romans, blinding the latter to the united front mounting against them.

As for me, I was happier than I could ever remember. While sitting around the peat fire, burning low and glowing in the pit, there was always raucous laughter as the Draiochta and the Eirish traders talked of their trickery and devilment. The Romans reminded me of the Hellenes, and I told stories about the foolery of Zeus and the gods to much hooting and applause. It was joyous to share in the hilarity. Every night was like a homecoming.

The other matter that had brought a smile to my lips was Carnonos. He had been pursuing me since the gathering in the Sacred Willow Grove at Avalon. The age-old bond between us two Otherworld beings was as deeply entwined as the ivy growing in the forest. I had felt the pull of him the moment I sat between him and Cyrridwen. He had been leaving me necklaces made of feather and bone, feathers from his beloved blackbirds. I would find them hanging on branches in the woods and on wayside cairns along the paths I travelled.

One night, as I lay on a carpet of tender moss in the ancient woods of Brackloon, feeling the pulse of the Earth beneath me, Carnonos's giant stag appeared. He stared at me awhile through boughs laden with lichen. His molten eyes were as brown and luminous as those of his master. An excitation arose in me like a wave spiralling up in the ocean.

"I know you are here, too, Carnonos."

He began strumming his harp and singing a tune as he made himself visible. He was adorned with a torc of twisted bronze around his neck, the ram-headed serpents at each end sitting low on his collar bones. Necklaces of feather and bone tied to his waist swung like pendulums in time with the music. His long, dark, curling hair flowed out from under his crown of antlers. As he came closer, I could see the dark hair covering his chest like a shield, and the phallus stiffening between his thighs. I was utterly entranced by him, and he knew it.

"I thought you only sang to the slain, the ones you felled yourself? Is that your intention with me?" I joked.

He smiled as he sat in front of me and finished his song. It was a mournful ballad about two lovers who lived far apart. They could only glimpse each other in the mirror of the Moon. I savoured both the singer and the message, stirring in me a sweet vision of our coupling. I knew it would be played in the tune of ecstasy.

Our togetherness was like the flawless rhythm of his songs. He enfolded me in his muscular embrace, and I breathed in his musky aroma, pure manna from the Ancients. I had known nothing like it before. Nor had he. Carnonos was the very remedy to counter the brutish lust of the Hellenes, Zeus especially.

We stayed in the bliss of the untrodden woods, talking and coupling from moonrise to moonset, aware that the Faery realm and woodland spirits watched us all the while. To them we were a living sacrament to the Cosmos. I grieved when the time came for us to leave for Bealtaine, unsure if we would ever be back in these woods. I consoled myself with the Knowing that he would be traveling alongside me for a time. And I would cherish the moments, sweet as fragrant chypre, until the time came for us to part.

The Fires of Bealtaine

Carnonos and I journeyed in his chariot to the Hill of Uisneach on Eire for the fires of Bealtaine. Called the Breath of Desire in the Celtic Realm, they were held at the midpoint between the spring equinox and summer solstice.

"Wait until you see Uisneach," Carnonos said. "It is the Sacred site of Eriu, Goddess of Eire."

The magical site had sprung up from the Earth as the omphalos, the navel of the whole of Eire. As we approached the hill, I saw hundreds of mortals scattered around like tawny rabbits in the late afternoon sun. The special Earth point had pulled the little chariot in which we rode so strongly toward it that it seemed Carnonos's stag might plunge into its very core.

The Tuatha de Danaan hovered in their Realm waiting to greet us. Many others from the Realms joined us, too.

"We wish to show you the portal in which we dwell," Morrigan said. "We call it the doorway to the Five Mysteries."

It was joyous to be in the embrace of the Five Mysteries again, known to the Ancients from the beginning of time. It was the Eternal place of All Knowing, where the Akashic tablets for the Souls of Earth were stored. Many Moons of contemplation and ritual were needed to enter its Sacred Halls.

"Because of the mortals' reverence for the Sacred rituals, the black-robes have begun to use them in their ceremonies," she said, "reciting their own words instead."

Myrrdin shook his head in disgust.

"They seek their own glory, instead of the Sacred," he said.

I had foreseen that the Ancient Knowing of the Draiochta and the rituals of the peoples of the Isles would be the means of keeping Ancient practises and Dark Moon Knowledge alive on Earth in times to come. Each season they gathered to bestow gifts of gratitude for the glory of Earth's abundance. They observed and paid homage to the Sun and Moon cycles, and the Mysteries of Being. And they knew it was the union between the still, inner world of Knowing and the outer world of action that brought forth Transformation and new life.

Rays of light streamed toward us as the Sun set low on the horizon. Myrddin, Morrigan, and others of the Council of Draiochta had summoned fire to light their torches. The flares blazed high into the evening sky as they lit two towering piles of wood for the purifying rites of the Bealtaine fires. The scent of spruce saplings and rowan and hazel branches rose from the fire to herald summer's arrival.

The mortals sat in the firelight eating piles of cheeses wrapped in leaves. Jugs of wine suffused with dried mushroom powder got passed from group to group. They sang bawdy songs, playing on their horn pipes and crude gut-string harps. Lugh and Carnonos accompanied them on harps carved like the lyres of Mesopotamia. As the mortals grew drunk on the special wine, they ran fearlessly between the fire pits, shouting, cheering, and singing. Then they gave a little wine to their cattle to calm them down before running them between the fires to rid the cows of fleas and ticks—a ritual of protection.

Evening drew on, and the fires burned down to piles of glowing embers. Wearing masks of bulls, foxes, horses, and birds on their faces, and with animal skins draped over their shoulders, the mortals danced wildly. Delirious with lust, they threw off their masks and skins and copulated in the shadows on the ground. The fires raging within them were a fitting celebration of the Earth's fecundity.

"Are your passions roused as much as mine?" Carnonos whispered as we danced in circles around the great stone of Eriu. We laughed and flung off the mortal garments we'd worn to disguise ourselves, our nakedness glistening in the moonlight.

"It is unholy how they treat my people," Carnonos said, as we lay together afterward, his fingers languidly stroking my hair.

He was referring to the black-robes. They had been decrying the rituals of Bealtaine from their pulpits, shaming the mortals into seeing their coupling as wickedness.

"It is an unholy mystery how they treat themselves," I said. "Why do they deny the pleasures of their own bodies?"

"I heard one say it is because such urges take them down the road to hell."

I thought of Athena and Artemis and their pledge to remain unsullied by male-kind in the pantheon, seeking femina pleasures instead. That commitment I could see, given the gods' propensity to rule over them and violate femina. And they were not of mortal flesh.

"How can the black-robes be of service to mortals if they themselves do not honor the ways of Nature? They are severing their bodies from their very Soul. It does not augur well for anyone."

Carnonos bid me speak no more of it, but I puzzled over it all the same. Did the black-robes fear the power of the yoni and their desire for femina flesh? Or was it male-kind they desired instead, indulging their secret lust under the cover of darkness? They failed to see the rhythms of Creation in mortal bodies, interwoven as they were with the rhythms of Nature and the Dark Moon. The Wisdom of the Ancient Knowing would be lost if the edicts of the celibates held fast.

As daylight beckoned, the Bealtaine fires had dwindled away with the nighttime revelries. Mortals were busy gathering buckets of embers to take to their home hearths as protection. I sat by the stone of Eriu alongside Brigid, Goddess of the Hearth, watching as the mortals tied their bundles on the backs of their beasts.

"I am well pleased with this tradition," Brigid said, as she spread love and blessings over the mortals making their weary way home.

"Did you enjoy the festival?" she asked, with a twinkle in her eye as she glanced over at Carnonos, sitting cross-legged beside the Dagda, and looking as satisfied as I.

"I did," I laughed, taking her hand in mine as one friend to another.

"Then you must come to the Imbolc when the spring comes round again. It is the celebration I govern, and I would welcome you to stand at my side. There are others to attend before Imbolc, of course. There are all the moon festivals, as well as Lughnasadh. Morrigan wishes you to be her significant at Samhain."

"I am honoured," I said, feeling Lilith's nod of approval from the aethers.

After Brigid left, I sat alone in contemplation by Erui's stone. Lilith came to join me.

"You are mimicking mortal ways, I see," she said.

I could tell from her mischievous tone that she was alluding to my liaison with Carnonos.

"Are you envious, Lilith?" I asked.

Her laughter was so loud I feared it might set off a quake in the ground. The gods and goddesses of the Celtic Realm quickly gathered around, mistaking her wild guffawing for an urgent summons.

"Thank you for your presence, Lilith," I said to her to reassure the rest.

"Remember. Stay the course," was all she said, before disappearing again.

Everyone in the Realm smiled when I told them the reason for the laughter. Though they remained silent as they sat beside me, I could feel their rising fears. If Lilith was bringing reminders to stay the course, that could only mean there was more to come, much more. As I had drawn closer to the mortals and observed their daily lives, I knew these fears were alive in them, too. I had kept my own counsel, but the anxious eyes that sought me out told me I had not altogether succeeded in hiding my own disheartened thoughts.

The Eclipse of Awakening

After Bealtaine we travelled to the Temple Isles, swept along in Carnonos's chariot over the windy seas and around the tip of Caledonii. We were headed toward the Isles of Orkneyjar, called Arcaibh by the Ancients, who had been drawn there since the time of the Atlanteans. They'd helped the Ancients build the tombs and henges there, the great standing stones set in harmony with the healing cycles of the Sun, Moon, and Earth.

"The Moon draws so close to the Isles I can see the markings on her face and feel her power to pull the seas," Carnonos said. "Brodgar, the place we're going, is like Uisneach," he added, "it lies on another of Earth's lines."

The legacies of Sacred Geometry were all over the northern Isles I visited. The Draiochta had been taught by the Atlanteans to follow the purifying lines on Earth that harmonized with the flow of the Cosmos. If only the mortals could see Eternity's Infinite Light as we could—a spiderweb of radiant portals weaving around the Earth.

As we circled the main Isle, I saw three formations below us that were a perfect replica of the group of stars the Hellenes called Orion's Belt. The Ancients in Egypt had called it the sign of Osiris. Ever-changing iridescent lights sang across the sky above us in greens, yellows, pinks and purples—it was the dance of Aurora's celestial music.

"Your friend, the Aurora," Carnonos said.

"Thank you, Goddess of Dawn and Dusk," I called out to my Ancient friend as we soared and circled in and out of the dancing waves of colour washing over us like a trance.

We landed beside the stone circle of Brodgar with the others, preparing ourselves for the Eclipse of Awakening. Sixty stones as large as the Gorgons encircled the Sacred space in perfect harmony. Every Realm was present. There were Faeries, Elementals, and the whole Devic Kingdom of Nature Spirits, as well as The Many and the mortals.

"We call these gatherings the Assembly of Middle Earth," Carnonos explained. "We have taught the mortals to measure the journey of the Moon from here, so they can watch the patterns of the skies to plant and harvest their crops. They see and honour these Realms."

We placed ourselves near the centre of the circle, nestling close to one another to enjoy the sight of the unfolding. The gathering was hushed in reverence as the Moon made its slow passage across the Sun and covered it in perfect shadow.

As the Moon journeyed on, the deep vibration of our communal humming opened the Wisdom portals of the Cosmos. The mortals fell to their knees, weeping with veneration. I had expected to be transported to the Otherworld in peace and rapture, but instead, I heard my own voice keening like the wounded.

The vision that had come to me was in keeping with Lilith's foretelling at the gathering of The Many on Avalon. I saw femina mortals in chains being hunted by rabid dogs and tortured by fire burning at their feet. Male-kind stoned them with rocks and threw them bleeding and broken into dungeons. It was as if they had been swallowed into the very bowels of Tartarus.

"What can this mean?" I cried aloud, shuddering at the horror before me.

I felt Morrigan on one side of me, Carnonos on the other.

"Come away," I heard her say.

They took me to a large pillar and sat me down behind it. The vision kept swirling around me in a vortex and, I couldn't catch my breath, as if I were drowning in an undertow. They chanted a low-pitched humming tune over and over, until I felt the pulse of the Earth beating beneath me again, pulling me back through time, shaken and confused. The ice and fire of Lilith was soon beside me.

"How do you do it, Lilith?" I whispered. "How do you cope with these bleak visions of Knowing?"

"I come from a realm far beyond the Earth galaxy," she said. "I understand the plight of mortal flesh and bones in different ways than you. You are deep feeling, one who knows their joy and pain. That is why you have been chosen as my emissary. You walk at the galaxy gates between the Realms of Earth and Heaven, gods and mortals."

At that moment, I would happily have traded places with her. Since my descent to Earth, I had known ecstasy and joy far greater than anything I had known before. Yet those moments were now mixed with the sorrow and torment I had hoped to leave behind in the pantheon. As I recalled the travails of the Underworld, Persephone's gentle face came to me, smiling her young but wise smile.

The vision reminded me that I must hold my ground and stay the course as Lilith had advised.

I made a silent vow. There was to be no more slipping into paroxysms of grief. If I were to help Lilith guide the Souls of the mortals back to the Divine Femina, to the Infinite Light, and support them through the dark times ahead, I needed to hold the might of Cosmos within me. My honey-mead Moon time with Carnonos would soon draw to an end. I had work to do.

Lammas (Lughnasadh)

The Ancient ritual of Lammas was the first of the harvest festivals—the celebration of ripened fruits and grains. Sheaves of wheat and oats were propped up together for the millers to grind into flour. Others were busy boiling barley wine in cauldrons. The smell of bread baking in the oven fires was all around us. Fresh-picked apples and pears in reds and greens spilled from baskets beside the mortals' dwellings. The rich bounty of the harvest was greater treasure to the mortals of the land than all the Queen's gold.

Cyrridwen, Goddess of the Grain, presided over the occasion, casting her magic over the bounty to keep it safe from vermin and disease. The survival of the mortals depended on their crops being ready at the right time, and on the careful storage of their produce, or they'd starve and die during Earth's long winters. Her presence at the festival also assured that the merchants and traders whose eyes were glazed with greed did not exceed their share of the goods.

The Lammas celebration was also known as Lughnasadh, named for Lugh, the master tradesman. Lugh revelled in the occasion, walking among the crowd, praising the crafters who displayed their wares for all to see and buy. He played his harp and sang for them, changing the words of their old songs to make fun of the crafters, himself included. Some of the others sang, too, and told stories to rival Lugh's, making us all cry with laughter. I laughed as much at Lugh's donkey bray of a laugh as the stories themselves.

"Will you help weave the dolls of protection with us?" Carnonos said, sharing dried leaves and stalks from the tall corn plants among The Many and me.

"I bless the dolls, and then we give them to the children," Cyrridwen said, ignoring the scowling faces of the black-robes as they walked by, inspecting our magic.

At the Lughnasadh ritual of handfasting, the tying of the knot, young couples had their wrists tied together with ribbons. It signified their intention to make a solemn vow to each other after thirteen New Moons had passed. The ritual of handfast binding was performed by one of the elder Draiocht. It was as momentous an occasion for the young couples as making their final vows.

The black-robes made a show of their disapproval, tsk tsking and shaking their heads, flapping their sleeves like rooster's wings while they ranted and raved. To their dismay, no one heard or heeded them. The priests were baffled by it. Unbeknown to them, I had conjured a spell to surround them with a cage and turn their words into animal noise.

"Would you care to tie the ribbon with me?" Carnonos asked. "The mortals celebrate me as the Godhead of Nature, the Green Man. Together with you, dear Goddess of the Dark and Light Moon, I believe we'd make a fine pair."

His proposal touched me deeply. I would have happily tied myself with him for all Eternity. But we both knew the time was drawing close when I would be leaving the beloved Celtic Realm.

"Thank you, my Love," I said, "but I must stay unbound to fulfil my calling in the Cosmos."

My sorrow at the thought of our parting made my heart sink like a stone dropped into the ocean depths.

"Come," he said, taking my arm. "We must watch the games. They will cheer you."

The games at Lughnasadh were as important to the mortals as the craft making and harvest blessing. Mortals came from far and wide to compete in the games, jostling, sparring and practising with each other until their chosen sport commenced. Wrestling was the first of them, followed by spear-throwing and running races. Cheering and clapping echoed around me as the victors' hands were held high; the losers were applauded just as loudly. Others were seated playing fidhcheall, a game of strategy Lugh had created using magical wooden pieces.

The merriment and joy displayed by the mortals on the occasion stood in sharp contrast to the mood of the sour-faced priests looking on from the side. The black-robes would have that same look about them when they stood before the mortals in the stone church in the morning. Knowing there would be a long night of revelry following the day's events, the black-robes had insisted that the mortals pray with them at sunrise. Green with envy at the success of Lughnasadh, the spiteful priests would shame and punish them with tales of the horrors of hell while they sat on their benches, dazed and heavy headed.

When sunrise came, I decided to join the mortals for the talk at the place of the one-god worship. Entering quietly with a veil on my face, I sat at the back, curious to hear the sermonizing. There were five of them standing at the front looking haughty and disapproving. I knew well that they'd named me a witch, condemned me as demonic. Lilith was construed as an evil serpent, so feared and dangerous that she'd been expunged from their holy book as if she had never existed. I longed to enlighten them. In truth, their creation story had begun in Mesopotamia. Lilith was Adam's first wife. She was his equal in Sacred Creation and had long been more powerful than any man-god. But I knew my words would only be falling on deaf ears.

A tremor rippled through the congregation as the tallest of the black-robes climbed the wooden steps to the pulpit and began speaking. His vehement words circled the room like vultures after prey. His face was creased with anger as he spoke, his lips twitching as he spat words from his mouth like rotten fruit.

"I will read to you from *Thessalonians*, chapter four, verse three."

He held the Bible close to his eyes, peering down his long, hooked nose to read the page. "And here it says: 'For this is the will of God, even your sanctification, that ye should abstain from fornication; that every one of you should know how to possess his vessel in sanctification and honour; not in the lust of concupiscence.'"

He looked up at the congregation, his teeth bared, snarling: "You must abstain from the immorality of fornication as we good men of God do," he said, extending an upturned palm to the black-robes by his side. "And the *only* place that you may be betrothed to one another is here in the house of God. God will judge the immoral and adulterous among you. Verse seven: 'For God hath not called us unto uncleanness, but unto holiness.'"

He shook a warning finger around the room. The young couples in the crowd with ribbons tied to their wrists flushed red and dropped their eyes in shame. The other mortals shifted guiltily in their seats, as if the red-hot coals of hell were burning beneath them.

"And further, I shall read to you from *Leviticus*, chapter twenty, verse six: 'Those who turn to wizardry and spiritists, and play the harlot after them, will be cut off from the Church and from their own people.'"

He raised his chin defiantly and looked straight toward my veiled self with a fixed and unholy stare as if he knew I was sitting there.

"Any man or woman who is a wizard or spiritist among you must be put to death. We must stone them to death. The blood of sin is already on them. Their blood will be on their own hands, not the hands of the innocent."

The mortals clutched at each other in fright, waging a battle between their deep belief in the old ways and their fascination for the one-god who promised salvation from their fear and suffering. I wanted to split his wooden pulpit in two with a resounding crack and could have done, such was my rage. But I held off, lest it frighten the mortals even more.

"Liar," I called out instead, laughing aloud.

I sensed relief in the crowd, relief that someone had baulked at his righteousness and acknowledged their bond and birthrite to the Ancient ways of their land.

He scanned the room, desperate to see who had defied him. Sniggers could be heard in the congregation. With a wave of his hand, he gestured for the jittery quartet of young black-robes to begin singing a hymn. They were badly out of tune. It pained me to hear them abuse the Sacred music. Worse still, that the black-robe was blind to the beauty, Grace, and Mystery in their holy book. Instead, he poured the scalding oil of judgement upon the mortals, chastising them with tales of blame, guilt, and shame—the bygone edicts of warring conquerors. I had heard enough of it and slipped away in disgust to tell the others of the travesty I had witnessed.

As soon as Morrigan saw me, she called everyone together and we sat in our circle as I told them about the priest's lamentable sermon.

" ... And the awful rage in him at the rules not being obeyed, rules from another time and place," I said as I finished my account. "His rage was like a poison in his body. He writhed and spat the words he spoke, as if summoning a deamhan, not Divinity. There was no mercy, no Love in his words."

"We know," Morrigan said. "It is as we told you at the Gathering. And it is worsening. The harder the mortals try to cling to their old beliefs, the more the black-robes threaten them. And us. Their Sacred book is ripe with Ancient Wisdom, but the tales have been skewed to awaken fear instead. To control the people."

We nodded our heads in unison. Myrddin grumbled to himself before speaking.

"And they promise that a better world awaits them, giving them a vision of ease for their mortal selves to cling to. The Knowing in their Souls is being forsaken," he said, banging his staff on the ground in disgust. "The Romans told us that the leaders among the black-robes have more gold stored in their edifices than the mortal kings and queens. They have great power with their wealth. This has become their quest."

"No woman is permitted to be speaker of the one-god," Morrigan added. "What will happen to the Spirit and Soul of women-kind if there is no one to speak for them? Male-kind elevated and women-kind denied? Are they to remain servants and handmaids?"

I did not like to say what my vision had shown me. Because of their Divine gifts for Creation, femina would be forced into submission. Their childbearing and their Moon-time cycles of blood, which opened and wove the Ancient Knowings through their Being, had made them a menacing threat to male-kind.

"The Faery folk and Elementals will never let the mortals forget who they truly are," Rhiannon said. "Will you?" she asked, peering into the Otherworld.

All of the Middle Earth dwellers stepped into view and danced around her.

"Keep one eye above, and one eye below," Lilith said, appearing along with them. "That is how it will evolve. The mortals of the land will follow the one-god with one eye, but they will keep another eye open for all of you. The old knowledge is as much a part of them as the air they breathe. All of it is connected."

"Ah, it is the Truth on the path to the Light you speak of, Lilith," Morrigan said. "These are our old stories."

"Why do the black-robes seldom speak of the son of the one-god, Jeshua? Or Mother Mary? They are the softness and the Light in the harsh stories," Lugh asked.

"Good question, Lugh," I said. "Lilith and I spent time with Jeshua and his beloved mother Mariam, called Mary. We enjoyed long talks with them. They taught mortals to hear the parables as Grace for their Heart-Souls. But their honourable stories of Compassion and Love have been told and retold so often, the meaning of them has been all but lost."

I thought back to those impassioned talks. Jeshua's great love, the ineffable Mariam of Magdala, was also known as Mary. She had been defamed by the priests as a lowly mortal. In truth, she was a woman with Knowing equal to that of Jeshua. She was a Priestess in the Ancient Temples of the Theraputeae, as was Mother Mary. Like the Celtic Realm, the Theraputeae had been attuned to the Fifth Mystery and the Earth cycles, and they sought Love and Wisdom for their people.

As I reflected on this, I felt an overwhelming sadness about the disavowal and silencing of the Divine Femina and her Knowing.

Hearing my thoughts, Lilith turned to me and swept her cool soothing force over my suffering Soul.

"Some will speak of Jeshua's stories, some will seek the Marys," she said, instructing me along with my kin. "But many will follow the one-god book without seeing the Mysteries within it. They will not be shown, they will not be told. The robes have endowed themselves with the power of the Sacred, silencing this Wisdom in the mortals. The robes now govern the path to the Infinite Light, to the Sacred seed of Knowing. We must help mortals hold fast to the Divine Femina within their Souls, lest She wither away and die."

Everyone's spirits sank when Lilith vanished again. We knew she had spoken the Truth. Our only consolation was that the Realms would be remembered as she had said. I also knew that those who followed the rituals of Witchery, honouring Earth and Nature, and the Seekers of the Sacred Truth would be like my shining torches. Their Wisdom would guide the way for mortals to find their way home to the Infinite Light in their Souls.

Samhain

After Lammas, I travelled alone for a time, healing my dispirited self in a vigil of silence while deep in the sanctuary of the Otherworld. The time of reflection would prepare me for the next of the Celtic rituals—the Samhain. It was the time when the veils between the worlds fell away and the pathway to the Divine unfurled. I was eager to reunite with Carnonos and fly in his chariot over the sea to Eire for the evening of Samhain.

The Draiochta and we of The Many gathered at the source of the Boinne River to raft along the waterway with the mortals. We sang to the Goddess Boinne before leaving, asking her for safe passage to where the river curved around the Sacred Circle of Bru na Boinne, the setting for the Samhain journey.

Winter had set in, and mist and drizzle were our constant companions as we drifted along the river in quiet reverie. Ducks huddled together on the riverbank, and drops of water from overhanging trees fell on our faces, blessing us on our journey. There was none of the usual chatter and banter, all of us deep in our Being as we readied ourselves to commune with the Underworld.

I wanted to visit the Otherworld again, this time with a renewed sense of purpose, and to seek counsel with wise Themis once more. I wondered what she had gleaned from afar about what was taking place in Earth's Realm. I also wanted to commune with Demeter, Persephone, Hera, and Hestia in my Samhain journey. I knew Athena and Artemis would join them, and the chance to mingle with The Many and the mortals may be irresistible to Aphrodite. I knew Lilith would be in attendance. This was her time as much as Morrigan's and mine.

For the mortals, Samhain was the time to prepare for their Death and pay tribute to those who'd gone before them by inviting the ancestors and Spirit guides to be heard. It was the time of the Winter solstice, when their reverence for the Sun gave way to honoring the Wisdom of the Moon as it pierced through the darkness of winter.

"Here we are," Carnonos whispered, rousing me from my dreams. "The Bru na Boinne."

I stepped off the raft, gazing all around me.

The Bru na Boinne was a mound encircled by ninety-seven rounded stones engraved with symbols of the Middle Earth Realms. He took me beneath the giant mound where the ground had been hollowed out in the shape of a mortal woman's womb, the Sacred Womb of Rebirth. The underground passage leading into it was the birth canal to the chamber at its centre.

"It is a masterful construction," he said proudly. "The Mystery of it is far beyond the reach of the black-robed ones."

As the Realms and mortals gathered group by group, huddling together in the hush of the Bru's passage, Morrigan and I performed the rituals for their journey through the Darkness to their Transformative Rebirth. The mortals had been fasting for ten long days in preparation. The hypnotic aroma of precious valerian and mugwort oil wafted from burning lamps. We intoned words to open their Knowing as we drew the sign of the Goddess on their foreheads with myrrh. Then we anointed their eyelids to rouse their inner Seeing to visions of Wisdom, before taking our seats deep in the Womb of the Bru.

"The mist will lift in the morn, and the first rays of the Sun will shine through the opening at the top of the mound," Morrigan told me in their silent tongue. "The rays streaming into the centre of the Womb will light the stone of Birth and Creation, the yoni. The wavy lines of Eternity will light up next to remind us that Death is but a new beginning. When the light touches the spirals in the stone, we are on the path to the centre of Transformation, the Lemniscate."

As the journey began, the first rays of sunlight on the stones gleamed like Atlantean quartz, lasting only moments before it disappeared again.

"Now we open to the darkness of the shortest day and longest night while we pass into the Underworld," Morrigan explained. "We stay here until the rising new Moon on the morrow shines on the stone in the same places the Sun has touched."

The profound Darkness brought visions of death and dying and memories of what had been, as well as visions of Rebirth and renewal to prepare the mortals for what was to come. Although Morrigan and I were there to guide them, the initiation was terrifying for some of the new-comers among the mortals. They cried out, and their limbs shook convulsively as their deepest fears manifested in tormenting visions, encircling and enveloping them in the darkness.

We waited alongside them until their Wisdom transformed their fears into lucid Spirit guides. We listened as they murmured to their guides and ancestors, seeking to understand the Mysteries they had encountered, the sufferings they had endured, and the Seeing of what was in store for them. It was the spirit quest that Demeter and Persephone guided at Eleusis, where mortals would come to see Death as the last Great Mystery, as a celebration and homecoming, not the dreaded finality they feared.

When the faint rays of the dawn Moon woke them again, Morrigan gave the mortals a potion like that of the Sacred Kykeion of Eleusis to break their fast and strengthen their Knowing of the connectedness of all things. She then cleansed and blessed them, particularly the youngest and the babes, scooping rainwater from the stone bowl set in the alcove; the tiny opening in the wall above allowed just enough raindrops to trickle in and fill the bowl between one Samhain and the next. She sprinkled water over their foreheads. The Ancient Cauldron ceremony of Birth and Rebirth had been stolen by the black-robes to use for their own birth blessing.

The older mortals and the rest of the Realm walked over to the ceremonial ponds, shaped in two entwining circles. It was the symbol of Infinity, another legacy from the Atlanteans. There the initiates immersed themselves in the cold water among the singing swans, the Ealie, the exalted birds from between the worlds. As they left the pond, naked and shivering, the recreated mortals made their way to the great fire nearby.

They wrapped themselves in furs and hugged each other to keep warm as they stood beside the blazing flames of the fire. Sparks flew upward in the night air, dancing with the sprites and fairies all around us. The mortals hung garlands of mistletoe around their necks to protect themselves from unwanted spirits lurking about after Samhain. The Draiochta revered mistletoe, cutting it from their sacred Valonia oak at the beginning of winter to give to the mortals to hang over their doorways to keep deamhans away.

The portals between the worlds were still open and clear at Samhain, and no libations were allowed, so as to prevent after-visions from befuddling the mortals in their altered state. They nestled together as they stared into the fire, their eyes looking inward at memories of what they'd seen and where they'd been. Their young ones were curled up between them, wrapped in furs and sleeping like caterpillars in cocoons.

"Did you commune with your other Realm?" Morrigan asked.

I shook my head. "I was too busy witnessing and holding everyone else's visions to make room for my own."

Morrigan chuckled softly. "Me neither," she said. "For the same reason as you. Happens every Samhain. I make sure everyone is calm and settled, then I return to the Bru alone for my own vision time. Would you care to join me?"

We crouched down to go back through the passage into the Bru—and in perfect timing. The Sun's first light penetrated the opening above, lighting the stone at the heart of the Womb to guide the way through the passage for us.

We sat close enough to reach each other if needed and far enough apart to create our own journey through the darkness. As soon as I closed my eyes, a vision was waiting for me. Flames leaped in front of me like the fires of the inferno in Tartarus's abyss. The terrible heat raged through me like a scalding venom. It was as malevolent a vision as I had ever seen. I knew I had to ride out the wave and not reach for Morrigan.

Like my misery in the Otherworld after the fall of the Hellenes, I knew this was another suffering I must withstand. I had already seen the horrors that awaited the enlightened femina and male-kind who dared stand up against the powerful. If I was to incarnate and be alongside the enlightened ones, I had to learn resilience in the lowest pits of the hell-world, or I would collapse and disintegrate on Earth. I pledged to be a beacon of Light and rise with the Moon on the mortals' blackest nights, offering the promise of Transformation for their Hearts and Souls. Dark Goddess Lilith inhabited the unknowable places. So, too, would I. I felt my Eternal Calling rise and rise in me, like the mountains rising from the oceans when Earth was made. Themis came to me as my commitment to the power of the Dark Moon was resounding through the aethers.

"Dear Themis, you are here," I said, embracing her in spirit.

"You have travelled far, Hekate. I see you have undertaken your own Transformation," she said. "Just as mortals must learn to do. You have reconciled your Heart-Soul. You have found the Balance of Harmony in the union with Carnonos. You have embodied the Alchemy."

The words she spoke rang with the Truth of sublime Wisdom. At last, I had become the Ancient Bridge, a Way-shower between the chthonic world and the inner Knowings of mortals, as was my destiny.

"Remember that Right Order and Justice is the way to overthrow the tyrants and put an end to their destruction. And defeat the greed-mongers. To give new life to the Ancient Divine Femina we must embrace the wholeness of Unity—the Solar and the Lunar, the Light and the Dark together as One."

Although she spoke in abstract ways, I knew the gist of what she was saying. Masks of difference placed on male-kind and femina had destroyed the Harmony by keeping them apart from one another. They had been made into warring opposites, pulling each other out of Balance. I thought of the Ancient Realms in the far lands of the East and their exquisite symbol—two swirling teardrops in a circle embodying the union of opposites.

As Themis left, Athena's tawny owl flew into my vision and Artemis's hounds came bounding toward me, followed by the Goddesses. The three of us embraced and danced together with our arms around each other's shoulders like a trinity of old.

"I have brought you two wolf-dogs as your Keepers," Artemis said, as two black dogs emerged from her pack and bounded up to me.

One dog's coat was as sleek as a panther's, his huge paws and jaw reminding me of Vanagandr, the wolf of the North. The other was a black-eyed woolly dog who nuzzled into my lap as if she'd always known me.

"They are yours to name," she added.

A Sacred Owl as white as snow descended in front of me, gazing at us with its opaque yellow eyes. I recognised it as Lilith's Keeper, separated from her in the aeons of time.

"I have brought her home to you and Lilith," Athena said.

Tears of gratitude slid down my face as I communed with the three new additions to my world. The young Goddesses had been shown that I would need companions in the times ahead, Keepers with special eyes and senses to guard and protect me during times of uncertainty. Athena and Artemis spoke of their frustration over the twisted tales told about them. His-stories had ensured that the gods would triumph over the Goddesses in the ancient myths and male-kind would prevail.

"We all know the Truth," I said.

"And we will endure," they added as they departed.

My dear companions Demeter, Hestia, and Persephone appeared in my vision state, and we embraced with tears of joy.

"Hera sends her love," Demeter said. "She is still caught in her attachment with Zeus. Yet she remains committed to keeping femina strength alive in the memories of the pantheon."

"And what of Aphrodite?" I asked.

"As you would expect. Hephaistos suffers while she pursues her own pleasures," Hestia said. "But she is a staunch ally for Athena and Artemis with her old Knowing of the ways of Love and warring."

I sent Aphrodite my greeting and gratitude in our Ancient tongue and she responded in kind. Traces of moonlight began threading their way into the vision space. I willed the light to wait until I'd had my fill of my old companions. Lilith obliged me with a cloak of darkness when she came to join us.

"And what of the Underworld?" I asked Persephone. "Do the mortal Seers and Knowers sense your presence there?"

"Hades tries to hold the reins of change strongly in his fists. But I make changes that rival Hermes's stealth and cleverness. Dionysus too is a great support, as he transmutes my visions of the Underworld into elixirs and intoxicants for the mortals. Most of them are spared from entering the bowels of Tartarus."

I made the ancient sign of the dove on my forehead, happy to see the proud faces of Hestia and Demeter on either side of Persephone, and Lilith standing behind them. Moonlight slowly filtered through the opening in the mound while I spoke to them of my plan for keeping both the Infinite Light and Earth's Soul alive for the mortals. I would summon rituals in the cycles of the Moon from the Celtic and the Ancients Realms.

As light shone on the crystalized stone of the Womb and my old family faded away, my whole being brimmed with gratitude for them. In the true spirit of Samhain, I had visited the past and the future all at once. Before emerging from the Womb, Morrigan and I blessed each other from the baptismal font, and then we stepped outside to the Dawning Raven Moon.

Carnonos and the Dagda had sat outside the Womb while Morrigan and I travelled through the portals of time. My Vanagandr wolf-dog startled Carnonos by running out ahead of us and going straight for him like a long-lost friend. I decided to name him Nonos, in homage to my dear companion, and the other Diona, after my loyal god-son Dionysus, who kept alongside Persephone.

"I have no need for such sentiment," the snow-white Sacred Owl informed me. "I am named Lilit, Lilith's Keeper of old."

Lilit was a shapeshifter. I watched as she changed from white to tawny brown to crow black and flew into an oak nearby, bereft of its leaves. Although I could feel her presence, I could barely see her black form blended into the shadows. Only her flaxen eyes were visible. Her powerful cosmic vision was legendary. Like Lilith, time was of no consequence to her. I wondered whether Lilith had a hand in bringing Lilit into my sphere. Right on cue, Lilith reappeared, communing with her Sacred Owl in a language older than any I knew.

"Is she to be your eyes and ears, Lilith?" I asked.

"She is our eyes and ears, Hekate, and much more besides."

My two new wolf-dogs went to Lilith as if they were hers, too.

"I thought you might be behind all of this," I said, regretting the words as soon as I had spoken them.

She and Lilit both looked at me with the same opaque stare.

"They will serve you well, as they did me."

Carnonos, Morrigan, and the Dagda had gone over to sit by the mortals' fire. The woodpile from the previous night had burned down to coals that glowed like rubies in the gold-blue flames. Some of the mortals had already gone home, while others stayed to consult with Morrigan and me as to the meaning of their visions and dreams. We listened and talked with them from moonrise to moonrise, guiding them to find Truth from within their own Wisdom.

These were the gifts that would be lost in the Great Change, the gifts of inner Seeing and Wisdom that came from the mortal's visioning and ceremonies. I knew the mortals would feel an emptiness and a longing in their core when this legacy of their Being was forsaken. I also knew the black-robes would ensure that it was.

Stories of Divine male-kind scribed by mortal male-kind would prevail, while unsung femina Divinity would sink into dark silence for thousands of years. The one-god and the sacrificial lamb Jeshua were to be the mortals' consolation for the loss of their Heart-Soul Knowing. At least they would have that.

Those taking the inner journey of Samhain would continue to embrace Witchery. The hidden teachings in the holy book of the one-god would be discovered and embraced by a few enlightened Souls. But my visions had shown me that most mortals would seek opiates and diversions to deaden the pain of the yearning and emptiness felt in their Hearts and Souls. When sitting in reflection beside the glowing embers at Samhain, I found a name for the impending loss of the Divine Femina. I called it the Great Disconnect.

Imbolc (Brigid's Day)

As a Dark Moon Goddess, Samhain had been my new beginning, my Rebirth. But for the mortals and Realms, it was Imbolc, the ewe's milk of new life, that was the Rebirth celebration. The Realms also knew it as The Return of the Light. Pink and white buds blossomed in the spring woods, filling the air with sweetness and joy. The bleating of newborn lambs and calves could be heard in the green fields around us, and the warmth of the sun seeped into everyone's skin like Ichor, the honey-gold nectar of the gods.

Both Imbolc and Lammas were important occasions for Carnonos in his role as Green Man. I watched as he handed out carefully tended saplings for them to make new hedgerows and shelters, and replace trees felled by the winter snows. I had not seen him since Samhain, when my Keepers and I had left the Realm's portal to journey all over the Earth in preparation for the next round of my existence.

Although we recoupled like a pair of starved rabbits, unable to leave each other alone from one moonrise to the next, few knew of our liaison, save the Draiochta and the Many of the Realm. Apart from tending to our bored and restless Keepers, we remained largely unseen and forgotten in our Otherworld domain.

During this time when the sap ran high, Brigid, Goddess of Fertility and Goddess of Imbolc, was alight with a secret love of her own. One velvet blue twilight she came to seek me out in my honeyed-mead time in the woods.

"Are you there, Hekate?"

I emerged from the thicket like a drowsy-eyed bear coming out of its winter sleep. I was curious to know why Brigid had sought me out. There were many wise ones in her own realm, particularly Morrigan.

As if reading my thoughts, she said, "Hekate, I am entangled in a bind I dare not speak of with my kin."

I studied her carefully. Her whole Being was dancing, and her eyes were as bright and green as the shamrock cape she wore. Her secret smile said all that needed to be said.

"There is someone I wish to have for my betrothed. Bres is his name, but he is not of my kith and kin. He is of the Formoire people, who are out of favour with my own, the Tuatha de Danaan. The Dagda will disown me if he finds out."

I knew the Formoire well. They were from the Underworld, including the Underworld of the oceans in the Celtic Realm. Brigid was right, the two peoples did not see eye to eye. They had fought a battle for the status as the Civilisers of the Celtic Realm; a battle the Tuath De had won. The history of enmity between them was long.

"Tell me about Bres?" I said, waiting for the Wisdom voices of Themis and Lilith to arise within me.

"Oh," she sighed, her face earnest with maiden love. "He is kind and thoughtful, and he does not agree with his elders that war is necessary. He is their new king, and he believes in a different way for the Realm, as do I."

Carnonos rustled through the trees into view, uncertain as to whether he should present himself. I gestured for him to stay silent.

"His people call him Bres the Beautiful. He looks like a changeling among them," she continued. "He is a giant, but he is so handsome, with such softness about him."

Lilith sent a puff of wind across my cheek to let me know she was there. She spoke in the silent old tongue lest Brigid could hear her.

"You see as I do," Lilith said to me. "It is time for the Formoire and the Tuath De to make a bond between them. These two will see that it happens. They are to be the reincarnation of the Ancient Rite; the Sacred Marriage of the Goddess with the King of the Land."

Lilith then disappeared as quickly as she had come.

"Was that Lilith?"

Brigid was as quick-seeing as Persephone, with a Wisdom beyond her maiden years.

"It was," I said. "We are agreed this is to be your destiny. Both of you will need much courage and strength. After you tell your kin of your intentions, for they're as clear to me as the waters of the brook, your every move will be watched and weighed."

"This we know. Our task is to unite our people for the greater good of Eire."

Although I did not see the Titanomachy of the Titans and the Olympieions in their future, the great clouds that hung over the match augured an arduous journey for the two of them. Telling the Tuath De and the Formoire of their intention would be daunting enough to start with.

"If I have your and Lilith's blessing, I will stand with the courage of the Oak so beloved by the Draiochta."

As I embraced her, I could feel her strong resolve. The powerful headiness of true love would spur her onward.

"The Many have already gathered for Imbolc. I will make my announcement to them tomorrow at the midday sun," she said before gliding away.

Imbolc celebrations commenced before the sun's first rays rose on the horizon. Brigid led the procession of the mortals and The Many as we circled around The Well of Plenty with our torches aloft, walking in the same direction as the Sun on its journey. We chanted to receive all the blessings of spring. I was aware from the prickling on the back of my neck that the Formoire had joined us. They were led by a young Formoir with a fine-featured face whom I presumed was Bres.

The mortals shuffled around the holy well, glancing anxiously over their shoulders at the towering beings that stood behind them. The Dagda did not acknowledge the Formoire but held his harp and log mor, his magic staff, like a war club and a shield before him. Morrigan stared at Bres, piecing together what might be taking place.

The fire from the night before had been smoored and covered with ash for Myrrdin and Morrigan to look within it for omens at first light. Everyone waited in suspense at sunrise, hushed in reverence as yellow-white rays fanned the sky and the patterns in the ashes became clear to the eye. Myrddin and Morrigan invited me to scry their meaning with them. A circular mound of embers still burned bright from the night before, a sign that a momentous change was upon them. They hesitated before saying anything aloud, looking to me to confirm their Knowing. I nodded.

Brigid had been watching us with eyes as keen as those of my Keeper Lilit. She seized the opportunity to speak her Truth in the early light, rather than wait until the sun's high point at midday. Bres came to stand beside her.

"Peoples of The Many, the Formoire, and the mortal folks, hear my words on this day, the most momentous of our Imbolc days," she began. "I bring you word of a great change in the way of things."

Morrigan moved to stand beside the Dagda, Brigid's father; the Truth of what was about to unfold was becoming apparent to all.

"I have chosen Bres of the Formoire as my Troth of Union."

"And I have chosen Brigid of the Tuatha De Danaan as my Troth of Union."

The two joined hands as a gasp of surprise arose from the gathering. Brigid continued, her voice calm and steady.

"We seek to join the old with the new, to be the living bridge between our two peoples, so that we may all know peace and fairness in our time. No more war. No more sorrows."

Her words, sourced in Love, rang with sincerity. It was plain that the union of Brigid and Bres had stirred up the ancient battle between those holding to the old ways and those wanting change. Some of them, mortals and immortals alike, slowly nodded as the new vision for lives of unity emerged before their eyes. Others glared and thundered harsh words at their opponents, unwilling to let go of beliefs as deep-rooted as the Fearnog, the alder trees of Eire. Some of the elder Tuatha De Danaan and Formoire remembered the warring as if it were only one moon past, the bitter memory of it swilling around like rancid ale in the mouth.

The Dagda clenched his jaw with anger. He saw his daughter's public announcement as a betrayal of her loyalty to him as well as to their kinship with the cherished Tuatha De Danaan. He regarded Bres, the new King of the Formoire, with distrust and suspicion, believing him intent on enslaving all of the Tuatha De Danaan as retribution for their victory over the Formoire.

"We, the Draiothe and The Many, shall talk before any decision is made," he announced.

"This is not a decision to be made for me," Brigid said, holding her gaze on the fire. "As Goddess and forthcoming Queen, I make this decision for myself."

All was hushed. Not a creature stirred. The birds had stopped singing, and even the vines of the forest paused in their eternal twining. I felt the presence of Lilith brush past me, remaining invisible amid the thorny tension of the gathering. Suddenly, the sound of Brigid's whistle broke the spell. She held her arms aloft.

"I have a poem to speak today," she said, with a poised and confident show of leadership. "After it, we shall read the smoored ashes once more, so that we may uphold the new vision for the seasons ahead."

To hark the water, we must bathe in its icy promise,
To hark the earth, we must taste its darkened soil,

To hark the wood, we must listen to its forests,
To hark the fire, we must breathe with its flames,
To hark the wind, we must soar with its tempests.

"This day we give blessings to all the Elementals, to all those who care for Eire, for us. This day we give blessings to each other, for our differences and our sameness. This day we give blessings to all the Realms, here and afar. This day we give blessings to all in all."

I moved toward the ashes, prompting Myrddin and Morrigan to do the same. We spoke together in the silent tongue so the mortals would not hear us.

"Lilith and I, Ancient Goddesses of the Light in the Dark Moon, give our Blessing to the Transformation."

"So be it," Myrddin added.

Much depended on Morrigan's response. She was the Seer for both Brigid and the Dagda.

"The division between old wounds and new love is here at Imbolc, both are alive today," she said aloud. "One is for the remembering, and one is for the healing. We will not forget the troubles endured. We must not, lest we repeat the conflict. It is now time to forge new irons in the Imbolc fire. I sanction the union of Brigid and Bres, and may they be blessed with the fruit of their loins and the spirit of Imbolc for many cycles to come."

The celebration was not filled with merriment, but as the wind rose and blew the ashes away, the great ring of fire revealed itself. Everyone knew it to be the sign of unity, the new bond of alliance that had been created. The revelation gave Brigid and Bres wings of hope for their future.

"There will be those who do not wish us well," Brigid whispered to me later. "We know this. But what we do is not just for Bres and me. It is truly for the sake of our beloved Eire, and for that, we will be as bound together as the Doire Knot."

Brigid, like Persephone, had understood that her role in the Cosmos was greater than her own existence. These were the moments that made my time in the nigredo, the Dark Transformation, worth bearing. They inspired and reminded me to keep seeing far beyond into Eternity. Brigid and Bres had become the Red King and White Queen of the Ancient tales of Alchemy in the Celtic realm. They had joined forces to create a new era for their people.

There was yet much to learn about the Celtic realm and its rituals, but I had already been too long in its bosom. It was time for me to go, to continue on the path of my destiny. I went to see Carnonos, my virile Green King of the Otherworld, who had sensed my imminent departure. We did not speak of it, but the wrench of our parting would be painful for us both.

I bade farewell to my other dear friends as well, then slipped into the temporal aethers to ready myself for my immersion with the mortals. Once truly immersed, I would be as bound to my ties with them as Brigid and Bres were to their Realm. I knew, too, that I would not remain invisible to the mortals once they had awoken to the plight of their indigo orb. For in the next dimension of time in the Cosmos, that demise had already begun.

PART FOUR

The Descent

Inanna of Sumer

Long, long ago, Inanna of Sumer, the Queen of Heaven and Earth, had taken me aside to share her Wisdom. She had endured the Seven Paths of Transformation, sacrificing her exalted status in the upper world to descend to the Underworld, where Ereshkigal dwelled, just as Persephone had done in the Hellene realm. Both had sought to restore the Divine Femina to the ambivalent Darkness of male-kind.

"To be among mortals you must learn to withstand unspeakable loss and pain, and you must be prepared to remain invisible to them as you do so," Inanna had said. "If you desire them to be who they are truly meant to be, you must help them go the core of their Being and see themselves laid bare, but without judgement. Therein lies the key to the Truth and the Light."

I was a young Goddess then, and I shivered at the daunting prospect.

"Love and Compassion for yourself and for others will be your greatest allies. Use them wisely. They are the supreme source for the inner strength you and the mortals will need for your Heart-Soul. The power of Love and Compassion has diminished in the conqueror world."

"Lilith calls the conqueror 'the go-between,'" I responded. "She also says that we need to have both the instinct of the conqueror and the vision of Knowing in our

Heart-Soul, that they must have equal measure in us, and they no longer do."

I was filled with youthful passion, eager to repeat Lilith's words to Inanna as if I were her equal, rather than listen to the wisest of the wise. Lilith appeared with her usual immaculate timing to speak for herself.

"The conqueror go-between is but an emissary, a messenger, whose only purpose is to serve the Knowing of the inner world," she said, for my benefit. "Its role is to help mortals gain mastery of their deep Wisdom. But the emissary has become the master instead of the servant, usurping the Wisdom and stifling Creation. It is our task to remind mortals how to reunite the two, lest they lose their Heart-Souls."

I was grateful for the memory of these wise words spoken by my mentors. My Keepers and I slipped through the portals of time to be alongside the first mortal, who was called a witch.

Hadia of En-dor

Hadia of En-dor lived in the Jezreel Valley of the Hebrew lands. It was the male-kind of these ancient lands who had scribed the early stories told in the black-robes' holy book. The lands of Jezreel and Eire were as different as day and night. But the endless warring between the male-kind tribes of Jezreel was as common there as it was in Eire and everywhere else on Earth.

Hadia had become known as Hadia the Unwed, as she was avoided by suitors because of talk of her sorcery. Throughout her childhood, her mother had hidden her daughter in the folds of her djellaba until she grew too big to be concealed. Her doting father had insisted she was a gift from the Almighty, yet no man dared venture to their door seeking her hand in betrothal.

"I do not care that I am unwed," she told her mother one day. "I do not wish to have the rough hands of a husband on me, nor his rules to bind me. I cannot help what I see. Papa says it is a gift. I am glad of it. And I am not frightened. I have helpers."

I overheard the sweet music of this declaration on the day I first revealed myself to her as she sat with her eyes closed in prayer. She had been living in the world of dreams and visions since her earliest memory, flying to the far reaches of the Cosmos without knowing how to manage her gifts, until she came to the attention of Lilith and me. I had seen she was mostly at ease with her visions and the voices she heard, and when I appeared to her, she immediately knew I had come as a Way-shower. She spoke with me often after that, especially at times when her dreams grew dark and foreboding. We would call on Lilith, too, to read the symbols for the worst of them. Some of the sights came from the distant world of warring male-kind, far from the safety of her humble home and the stony path she trod to the village well.

She made potions with the Wisdom gleaned from her visions, knowing which plants and spices aided with birthing, which ones cured the maladies of mortals and animals. Villagers sometimes sought her out in secret for a potion for stealing hearts or mending broken ones. Suitors may not have ventured to her door, but as soon as her father went to tend to their goats, the femina of the valley would loiter outside her dwelling, waiting their turn for Hadia's elixirs and wise words.

One day, Hadia's mother came running home from the well, her goatskin bags still empty.

"Hadia, Hadia!" she cried, panting. "Hide the remedies—quick! The king's men are coming, and one has asked for you. They are in disguise, hoping to catch us."

Saul the King had been ordained by the famed prophet Samuel. After years of infertility and pleading to God, Samuel's mother had proclaimed him God's miracle when at last she had given birth to the child. She created a proud, spoilt son who grew up believing the story to be true. I had watched as Samuel asserted his right to choose who ruled their people, mistakenly believing his own opinion to be a decree from their one-god. Ever fearful of his prophesies being exposed as false by a true oracle, he banned necromancers from living in or visiting the kingdom. We

Otherworld dwellers laughed at his hubris, his adamant authority lending him a credibility he did not warrant. I wondered how the young King Saul had fared in his wake.

"Quickly!" Hadia's mother cried in panic as she heaved the stone urn aside to reveal the hole where they hid their money.

"Ama, it won't all fit in," Hadia said, digging frantically into the dirt and shoving as many tiny ampoules of oil down the hole as she could. She hid the rest under a bundle of straw.

A man's voice called to them from outside their doorway. Hadia wrapped a shawl over her head and shoulders, and stepped out into the bright sunlight, partly shadowed by four men. They were dressed in shepherd's garments, but she saw that their sandals were made of finest lambskin, not the tough frayed leather worn by shepherds of Jezreel.

"Who are you, and what do you want?" Hadia said. Her mother, who stood behind her, poked her in the back for her boldness.

"I wish to speak to the one known as Hadia," said the gentlest-looking of the men, his scraggly beard a sign of his youth.

"Why?" she said. Her mother poked her even harder, trying to keep her own mouth from trembling.

"It is your assistance I seek," he said.

"Please come inside," her mother said anxiously, as she lifted the rug over the entrance and gestured for them to come in.

155

Only one of the men stepped inside; the other three kept watch outside the door. Hadia sat down on a woven mat and invited the man to be seated opposite her. I whispered his name into the ears of her thoughts.

"So, you are Saul the King, I believe?" she said, ignoring her mother's wide eyes.

He sat before her, shy and fidgeting, unaccustomed to such familiarity.

"That I am."

"What is it you seek from me?"

"I hear you are a necromancer."

Hadia's mother looked at her daughter in fright. She bit the edge of her shawl and mouthed "No" to her.

"Surely only a fool would agree to such a claim," Hadia said. "Did not Samuel the prophet banish all such people from the kingdom?"

He nodded in agreement and raised his hand as if hushing a crowd.

"I come seeking such a person, not for punishment, but for guidance."

Hadia sat for a time, still and peaceful as a dove, and assessed his Truth.

"He brings woes heavier than the old stone urn, and already knows his destiny," she said silently to me. I summoned Lilith, sensing what the young king was about to ask her.

"You wish to speak to Samuel the prophet from his grave," Hadia said.

"How do you know that?" he asked, his face tightening.

She held his gaze with her soft almond eyes, weakening his defences.

"I do," he sighed, "although I fear I know what he will say. Our enemy, the Philistines, want war and mean to have victory, and I will die with my soldiers."

I had no desire for Hadia to summon the old prophet through her Knowing. He had been dismissive of the femina and brutal at times. And I did not wish her to deliver the fate that awaited the young king seated before her. Lilith took the decision off our hands by drawing back the veil between the worlds to reveal Samuel in all his glory. He rose into sight as a vengeful skeleton and pointed a dried bone of a finger at Saul. Hadia and her mother shrieked in fright. Saul clutched the side of his robe as if about to get up and flee.

Samuel's raspy words were harsh and accusatory: "You will die in the battle, and another king will take your place. I warned you that the Philistines must be stopped. You have been too weak."

Lilith shut the veil tightly again, stopping his vitriolic attack on Saul. We could hear his words echoing after him as he fell through the aethers to the farthest reaches of hell.

"If you believe this, then it shall be your undoing," Hadia told Saul, pained to see the king weeping before her eyes. "You must not believe his words, for they are his and his alone. You must listen to the words in your own heart," she said to comfort him.

"But these *are* the words inside my heart!" he cried. "It is as if Samuel still governs my every thought."

Hadia sighed, knowing as she did that Saul had set his own course. To soothe his despair, Hadia's mother offered him a cup of dried chamomile and valerian leaves steeped in hot water. Hadia loaded the king's soldiers with tinctures and oils to remedy the king, but all to no avail. Within the space of one Moon cycle, Saul and his army had been defeated.

Meanwhile, the word of his visit spread quickly, and villagers were lining up for fortune-telling outside Hadia's door, both femina and male-kind. But she turned them away, fearing retribution.

"Our lives could be the price we pay for seeing the king's fate, let alone anyone else's," she told me.

"But it was Samuel who decreed Saul's fate," I countered. "That dead man's spiteful words burrowed into the thoughts he had already carved in Saul. He was unable to hear his own voice behind the loud decrees from Samuel he had heard all his life."

"I know this to be true, Hekate," she said. "And the people of my valley believe this, too. But I also know I do not wish to become a Samuel. My gifts could turn me into one like that."

Lilith and I comforted her distress as best we could. We reminded her of her innate goodness and humility, the very opposite of Samuel's nature, but the event had shaken her too deeply. She went on making the healing balms and remedies. But she refused to be consulted as a Seer ever again.

"Another silenced one," Lilith said as we hovered above the rooftops, knowing it was time for me to leave.

We had seen ahead, in the written stories of male-kind, that Samuel, believing he alone could hear the word of his god and, bloated with self-importance from childhood to death, would be lauded as a prophet. While a village girl who had visions of pure Knowing, a true Seer and Healer, had to hide her gift.

"The Witch of En-dor is how Hadia will always be known, a faceless, nameless Witch. She will be a part of the long legacy of femina who carry the burden of fear that their very gifts might put them to death," I said to Lilith, determined not to slip into despair.

"Men of power will seek Witchery and Wizardry when the Cosmos does not align with their wishes and desires," she said. "The true Seers and Knowers will walk on Earth at their peril."

There was no one to enlighten the conquerors about the pretenders to Witchery and Knowing, charlatans who would tell them what they wanted to hear rather than make them taste the vinegar of Truth. The pretenders maligned the role of true Seers and Knowers, drawing wrath and condemnation from the powerful and the ignorant among the mortals. But the silencing, torture, and persecution could not erase the Sacred Wisdom writ in the bones and blood of mortal Seers and Knowers. It was as well that Lilith and I made sure of it. There was worse to come.

Malleus Maleficarum (Hammer of Witches)

Lilith and I decided that in my next descent to Earth I would go back to visit my beloved Celtic kin in Eire, where mortal Draiochta followers had been hunted and burned, their Sacred Groves cut down, and memories of their Realm driven deep behind the veil. They greeted me as if I had never left, merely shuffling to make a space for me at the hearth as they always had. Carnonos circled his arms around my waist and held me close. The Draiochta were as faded as Lilith and me, looking pale and colourless as old husks. There was gloom in our reunion, an unspoken hollowness where fullness had been.

"I have heard tales from a book describing their hatred for femina," Brigid said as we pressed together. "*Malleus Maleficarum*, the hammer of witches, it is called. The book was writ with the ink of loathing. It is their account as to the basis for the burnings."

"What likeness of man writes such a book?" Myrddin asked.

"A man raised by the black robes since a child, one hungry for fame but fearful of the pleasures between a woman's legs," Morrigan said, ready for battle in her role as Badb the Crone. "He sees teeth in those hidden folds, eager to bite off his manhood."

Despite the seriousness of our talk, we had to laugh. She had spoken her Truth like Baubo, the bawdy trickster of old.

"He is a dangerous man who can convince the powerful red-robes of Rome of this story," Brigid said. "His deceitful words foment hatred and fear in others."

"It is yet another rendering of the conqueror story," I said. "I shall go back through the portal and visit this black robe at the time of his writing this book. Let us see how this animosity started with him. You are welcome to join me."

"Our people have already been tainted by his words," Myrddin said. "I have no wish to hear more of his foolishness, but I shall join you in support."

Lilit the Sacred Owl flew ahead of me, followed by my wolf-dog Keepers, Nonos and Diona, to the place of the black-robe Kramer. I had anticipated his form to be ugly and I was not wrong. His skin was sallow and sickly. Not a trace of pleasure gladdened his face; his coldhearted eyes were sunk in their sockets. A foul odour came from the celibate's sweaty black robes, his body unwashed for fear of releasing the milk in his loins.

Kramer paced back and forth in his room dictating words to a young scribe, who was writing feverishly to keep up with him, eager to please this unpleasable man. He stood over the scribe's shoulder, struggling to read the words through the mess of corrections and alterations. Shoving the young man aside, he took up the quill himself.

"Go," he said, dismissing him with a wave of his hand. "You have made too many mistakes. It is better I write it myself."

He spoke aloud to himself as he wrote, flipping through the pages of a great tome that sat on his desk—Witchcraft stories.

"The depravity of women. . . . Ah, here it is," he said.

"*Ecclesiasticus*, chapter twenty-five: 'There is no head above the head of a serpent; and there is no wrath above the wrath of a woman. I had rather dwell with a lion and a dragon than keep house with a wicked woman.'"

Each page in the Holy Writ was illustrated with engravings in curlicues of gold, red and blue. The mismatch between the ornate art and the words he chose was not lost on me.

"And I shall use this from Seneca," he said, splotching the page with drops of blood-black ink. "The tears of a woman are but a deception. They may spring from grief, or they may be a snare. When a woman thinks alone, she thinks evil."

To him it mattered not that Seneca was a writer of plays, rather than books on faith. Nor that his own arguments demonstrated an ignorance about femina that was breathtaking in its sweep. On and on he went, muttering as he wrote of women's slippery tongues, their feebleness of mind and body, and their many carnal abominations. His bald head bent lower and lower over the page as he scratched away with his quill, his jaw clenched with fervour.

"All witchcraft comes from carnal lust, which is insatiable in women. They are evil creatures with their filthy carnal acts," he spat.

He absently touched his phallus before catching himself and looked up guiltily, as if he were a novitiate about to be hit with a stick. He fought to suppress the urges that still prowled in him like feral cats. The temptresses that entered his dreams and raised his phallus could only be shape-shifting Witches—the Succubi, Satan's daughters. They teased and tormented him, reminding him of the punishments endured as a youth to cleanse his Soul of the devil.

"And they shall be stripped naked, and they shall be examined for the signs of a Witch. The hirsute body of the devil on them, warts and growths of skin on them, and the most telling sign of all—the third nipple to feed the devil's spawn."

His arguments were detailed and innumerable. Some were drawn from the testimony of women accused of heresy who had been tortured to madness, stretched on racks until their limbs tore from their bodies or whose boots were filled with boiling water as they screamed in pain.

Suddenly, his tone became mild and reasoning, his vitriol having been spent.

"They are faithless creatures by their very nature. If they were to resist their carnal urges, they would be given the grace of the Virgin Mary and remove the evil that Eve has wrought within them."

I exploded with laughter at his words, especially when I heard him recite this next bit of wisdom.

"No woman, other than Themis, has known philosophy and order," he stated aloud.

On hearing this, I summoned my kin from the old order to read what had been written. Themis came first. She looked over his shoulder and read the words, smiling her wise smile.

"He knows nothing of me," she said.

"Nor me," said Inanna, who was present in her incarnation as Eve.

Mary, Goddess and Priestess, mother of Jeshua, stroked his head in pity.

"In my name, he has made women either a virgin or a whore," she said. "He fears, too, that his secrets will be unveiled at the Second Coming, the Apocalypse of their biblical story. Compassion shall be his, for he knows not what he does."

"Why must the robes and others of this ilk force such beliefs upon the mortals? That, I do not understand," Myrddin added. "The mortals in our Realm were free to choose which gods and goddesses they envisioned and followed."

"It is because of fear and greed," Themis said. "Fear and greed are as much of a scourge for the mortals as they were for the Titans, the pantheon, and many others. They have long forgotten it is Love and Compassion they most need, not edicts and opulence."

We all fell silent under the heavy weight of her words, the Truth of it making us ache in our Souls.

"Lilith would tell us, 'It is simply the way of things,'" I said to break the silence. "That there has always been greed and the persecutors and victims that come with it. Witches, Hebrews, and the ones called Infidel Saracens.

The gypsies of the far east, too. Those with ebony skins, those with different ways. So many have been hunted down, herded, and executed for being different from the conquerors."

I looked into the depths of future portals and winced, stung by the Seeing.

"But this man's damning words will plague *all* femina for hundreds and hundreds of mortal years. The Priestess and Knower in them, The Seer and the force of the Healer in them will be crushed and hidden. Only a few will withstand it and prevail."

Then, off in a far distant portal of the future, I caught a glimpse of something I knew would bring joy to the hearts of my kin.

"And this I have seen as well," I said. "One day in times to come, an unwitting male-kind will make a joke to a group of femina. He will call them a coven, reminding them with a smile how Witches were once burned and tortured. And they will feel the powerful memory of it flash through them like silver lightning. Then one of them will look him straight in the eye and speak with the strength of a true Priestess of Knowing."

"*Yes*," she will say. "And we're all back."

Dame Alice Kyteler and Petronilla de Meath

I then travelled with my Celtic kin through another time portal to the fourteenth century in Eire, arriving in the province of Leinster. Beyond the wooded hummock where we made our bed for the night was the village of Kilkenny. The churches of the village rose high above the mortals' humble dwellings, offering them the promise of paradise. Bells tolled the hour from the towering steeples, reminding mortals of their duty and obedience to their faith.

When daylight broke, Carnonos, Morrigan, and I walked into the village. Peering inside the first church on the lane, I saw the Ancient Celtic cross and symbol of fertility on the walls and ceiling. And there on the cross hung Jeshua in crucifixion, forlorn and forsaken. Gold-covered altars as grand as the feast tables of the Hellenes stood at the front. It was there the black-robes delivered the sacrament as if they were gods themselves.

Next, we visited the church named for Saint Canice of Kilkenny. The carved wood beams in the arched ceiling looked like great wings flying up to heaven. The white stone arches underneath framed coloured-glass windows depicting stories from their Holy Book.

"It dazzles the eye," I said.

"The mortals are hoodwinked by the finery," Carnonos said. "Why can they not see the unevenness between their poverty and the riches of the robes?"

"It is clever trickery," Morrigan said. "They conjure a spell over them with their jewelled windows and their gold. They would have the mortals forget that they shit and piss and cuss, just like the rest of them. And fornicate, too, though it's forbidden."

We laughed together as if we were sitting at the fires of old. They knew I'd come to Kilkenny to whisper in Alice Kyteler's ear, a femina accused of Witchcraft. She had married four times, inheriting much wealth from each of her husbands upon their death. Slanderous rumours had been started by the stepchildren of her second husband. They said she had bewitched her husbands to rob them of their money. They claimed that her fourth and final husband, Sir John le Poer, had died of poisoning by her hand.

When I cast my eye over Sir John just hours before his death, I did wonder if Alice had dallied with the dark spirits of Tartarus. Clumps of hair had fallen from his head, and his brow was dripping with sweat. Sir John sat at his desk with a quill pen in his trembling hand, writing his last wishes. He put his will in an envelope, sealing it with yellow wax from the lands of the Far East. When he licked the sticky substance from his fingers, I knew it was not Alice who had been the poisoner. Deadly arsenic in his sealing wax had caused the demise.

I waited until the night of the Dark Moon to enter the realm of Alice's dreams. She was visioning the lost husbands who once had lain beneath her, fondling her breasts and gasping with pleasure. If sexual prowess were a dark art, Dame Alice was a mistress of its secrets. She had worn them thin satisfying their lust.

As she slept on, fearful phantoms arose in her dreams and came into my sight. Alice and her son were running frantically, chased by a man in purple robes. His garments were threaded with gold, and he wore a peaked hat as his crown. He was fat and bloated with a crazed look about him, like a bull in heat. I gently stirred her awake, knowing that terror from fear-filled sleep erupted as fire in mortal bodies. Her Dark Moon vision would prepare her for what was to come.

"I know someone is there," she said, sensing my presence as she awoke. "Do you mean me harm?"

She was not a Seer or Knower, but her senses were keenly tuned. I waited until she had lit the candle by her bedside, and then I conjured the shape of a dove on the heavy brocade curtains of her bedchamber.

"Oh!" she whispered, looking at the image before her. "Praise be."

Propping herself up on her pillows, she rubbed her eyes in case they had deceived her.

"I know someone is here to bring me aid. Are you an angel? I would desire to know your name?"

I whispered my name into the flickering light, uncertain if it would be familiar to her.

"Is it Hekate, you say? I do not know of your name," she said. "But I need the help of the very heavens. I shall talk and just hope that you hear me, for there is a monster in my dreams."

A tear slid down her cheek, and she wiped it away, rallying a weak smile.

"I shall tell you what has taken place, because I fear in my heart there is worse to come ..." She paused as if waiting for a word from me.

"I have not yet seen the monster in the flesh. But I know him to be the Bishop of Ossary," she said, grimacing. "I hear tell he comes from the inquisitions and witch hunting at Avignon. And that he has set his sights on me as his devil here in Eire, thanks to the lies of the ungrateful wretches born from the second of my husbands, Adam Le Blund of Callan."

She rubbed her eyes again, as if to rid herself of a sight she could not bear to see. The skin of her lovely face was as flawless as porcelain, but sleepless nights had darkened her eyes and hollowed her cheeks with shadows.

"You must think me a wicked woman with four husbands to my name, and a man of the cloth bent on shaming me for my lack of virtue. But I insist, I am not a Witch! I do not have the skills. 'Tis true I enjoy the company of male-kind. There's no denying it. I favor money as well. But I was wealthy in my own right by virtue of the fortune I brought with me when I wed. I learned the merchant trade from my noble parents. With money of my own, why would I murder my husbands and put myself at risk?"

She arose from her bed, plucking a wrap of fine-spun wool to cover herself, and sat by the dwindling flames of the hearth.

"My dear second husband, Adam Le Blund, was a clever moneylender. He left his fortune to my son William. Therein lies the trouble. Le Blund's kin cared only for his money, never working at his business nor bothering to visit him. They were as strangers long before he came to court me."

She poked at the fire with an iron, adding a few more lumps of peat. A gust of wind blew smoke down the chimney and into the room.

"Richard De Valle, the third husband—he left his wealth to me and my William in his will. So, you see how it is that we fell prey to jealous, small-minded gossipmongers."

She threw her head back and laughed. "Ha! The stories they tell! They say I have cut up animals and left their innards at the crossroads to Kilkenny. And they say I have stolen the key to Saint Canice, and there at the altar, I have placed fingernails and hairs from the buttocks of a man, and garments from unbaptised babes, and all manner of impossible things tucked in the skull of a robber. Some say I consort with a demon called the son of Art. Who is this creature, pray tell?"

I knew all too well the foolishness of which she spoke. Among witchery and other demonic notions they had of me, the black-robes and their followers had also dreamt me up as the sinister hexer at crossroads, and poor Nonos and Diona as my hounds of hell. We had only stood at the crossroads of inner journeys, gently guiding the way, but that way of Seeing was long gone.

"And this foolish man, this bishop, has believed their nonsense and wishes me accused—of heresy. They call these preposterous stories Witchcraft, as if the true Wisewomen of Witchery would engage in such nonsense."

She sighed with dismay. "What am I to do? A demon rules the bishop, for it is clear he has put the face of the Almighty on himself and the face of the Devil on me. I beg of you, bring me another sign like the dove of Almighty God to help me keep my faith."

I longed to say aloud which demon lurked in the bishop. But she knew as well as I about the desires of the flesh and how envy and spite could curdle the bile.

My Keepers watched as I slowly conjured the Light of a full Moon in her bedchamber. It was if her curtains had been flung wide open. Sacred Owl Lilit landed on my shoulder in approval and my wolf-dogs nudged my side. I had never evoked such a stunning phantasm.

Alice's startled eyes glowed green as moss. She stood up from her chair and spread out her arms, her shawl slipping to the floor. Tears rolled down her cheeks as she danced around the room, the floorboards creaking beneath her feet.

"She will endure," Lilit said, as if Lilith herself stood there beside me.

It was as well that Alice took comfort from the vision, for she would have much to endure. The Bishop was like a rabid dog in pursuit of her defamation and execution. She had become an unwitting pawn in the contest over who would have dominance in the kingdom—the black-robes with the powers of Rome on their side or the royal-robes with the powers of Eire on theirs.

The brothers of Alice's fourth husband sided with her. One of them was a sheriff, who denounced the bishop as "an ignorant, low-born vagabond from England." The other brother, who was the governor of the district, arrested the bishop. Their efforts mainly created theatre for the bishop, who paraded himself like a peacock in all his finery, his voice loud and imperious in their courts. His rage at Alice after his eventual release was all-consuming.

In the midst of the turmoil, I heard Alice call to me, wanting to share her thoughts aloud as she had when we first communed.

"I hope you are there, Hekate," she began, sitting on the edge of her chair. "For sadly, I must leave my beloved son and my companion, poor dear Petronilla, in Eire this very night, or else I will lose my life to the unholiest of men. I go to seek protection from the powers that be in London. But until I reach safer shores, they are in the jaws of a monster. Please, I beg of you, protect my son who stays to guard our trade. Though he is a man, I fear for his safety. He's done no wrong but be borne to me. And please save dear Petronilla, whom the Bishop has already taken prisoner."

She began sobbing, her body quaking with fear.

"Dear God, protect them please, I beg of you!" she said, with her hands clasped to her breast.

The Many and I had watched with sadness over the plot in which she had become embroiled. For me, it was yet another Titanomachy, the endless battle of wills as to who held dominion over whom.

I conjured the dove on her curtains again, hoping it would be visible to her in the moonlight. A soft rapping on her bedchamber door signalled it was time for her to go. Picking up a small bundle of belongings, she looked around her room one last time, pressing a hand to her breast when she spied the dove.

"Oh, thank you, thank you, a thousand times thank you," she whispered, wiping the tears from her eyes.

She swung a cloak over her dress and hurried to the door, where her son William embraced her, urging her to make haste. I knew she would be sheltered, but the Bishop's wrath hung over her like Damocles's sword. Further enraged by the escape of his quarry, the Bishop turned his attention to Alice's son, whom he cornered with threats and blackmailed into making bestowments to the Bishop's coffers. But young William Utlagh had too many friends in high places to become a pawn in the Bishop's game of revenge.

It was to be Alice's maidservant, the humble Petronilla de Meath, upon whom he would unleash a vicious fury of retribution. Arresting her of Witchcraft, he put her in jail and had her whipped day and night until the lash marks were festering wounds. Her screams of pain could be heard throughout the town, but no villagers dared protest on her behalf lest they be put to trial themselves. Alice's friends petitioned on Petronilla's behalf, but to no avail. The Bishop had found someone to punish, and he was not about to let her go.

"I swear by our Heavenly Father, Almighty God, there has been no devilment," I heard her say as she pleaded and begged for mercy, praying to the same god as the bishop.

Try as we might, with our best diversions and charm-work, The Many and I could not penetrate his madness. Nor could we protect Petronilla and save her from his cruelty. I sat alongside her through it all, grieving deeply for her, and more repulsed by what I heard and saw than by anything I had yet witnessed.

"Did you and Alice fornicate with Satan? Together?" he sneered, hissing the words into her ear. "Did you make potions from the blood of dead babies to bewitch men so you could seduce them? Did you take their entrails and place them at the altar of God?"

He ordered the torturers to probe her yoni with a rusty sword for signs of the devil, and to cut off her nipples, which he said had suckled the devil's spawn. Even though she read the scriptures aloud, while bleeding profusely, he insisted she was a witch and that Satan was trying to outwit them in their tests of witchery on her.

Finally, he had her whipped again until she screamed the confession of her and Alice's guilt in public, after which he had her burned at the stake. Her death left a permanent stain on us all. We mourned deeply for Petronilla and the abuse she had suffered. And at how powerless we had become in the midst of the depravity. We grieved, too, to see the tragic turn the mortals' world had taken, especially for femina.

Truth mattered little to the bishop and those who followed him. He had been maniacal in his attempt to assert his omnipotence in Eire. Accusing healers and midwives of Witchery would be his path to Rome. They were easy prey upon which to paint the image of Satan and gain the acclaim he so desperately sought.

The bishop was but one of hundreds of the black-, purple-, and red-robed monsters we had seen in our visions who, when freed from the laws of kings and queens, became perverted with power, terrorizing mortals into following their ways, or else meet the fate of the condemned.

Mother Mary was the only femina who had survived their campaigns. She was the last of the visible Goddesses to be worshipped. She had replaced the Black Madonna, whose statue was now shrouded in ivy on the winding byways of old where she once had reigned. But Mary, the Sacred One, the Womb of the Cosmos who bore the son of their god, could not be denied. It was her image, crowned in stars of glory with the Sun and Moon at her feet, that shone Light on the Knowers' third eye. And it was her Divine Love that penetrated and softened their hearts as she stood serenely gazing at them from shrines and colourful church windows.

Truth and Knowing were desecrated by the robes who sought to expunge Mary's sacred origins, along with the Dark Moon Wisdom lodged within mortals' Souls. The Mystery of the Divine Femina had been buried and silenced; yet it lingered like the eerie stillness that settles over an unvisited grave. Lilith's and my only consolation was that we knew they never could destroy her. The Ancient memories of her were as indelible as a mortal's thumbprint. And we would never give up our quest for her return.

The Sol Niger (Dark Sun)

The visions I had foreseen now gripped the lands all around us, as if Tartarus had risen from the primal darkness. This was the time of Sol Niger, when the intrinsic Knowings of the Moon had been eclipsed by the Dark Sun of pitiless male-kind. The Great Disconnect had taken hold on Earth. And all I could do was persevere through it.

I watched with an aching heart as the followers of the one-god faiths were consumed by wars for domination, and the reverence for Nature and the Otherworld had been forsaken on Earth. Great storms scourged the lands, and hapless mortals were swept to their death in raging torrents and floods, or buried in landslides and quakes. Disease was rampant, and villages and towns were overrun with vermin.

Of course, the robed ones had no answers for remedying the mortals' plight. They tried to lay the blame for Nature's catastrophic upheavals at the feet of the fallen angel Satan and his wicked followers, the Witches. Tales of evil Witches spread wildly in the mortals' towns and villages. Some said they clawed at the flesh of babies with their talons or ate them whole. That was said to be Lilith's legacy. They said Witches made their night visits flying on broomsticks smeared with blood. The healing art of Witchery by herb lore was looked upon as a curse instead of the balm it truly was. Few femina, if suspected of practicing the craft, escaped the tentacles of persecution.

"Lilith," I called. "Can you not put an end to this? I beg of you."

She emerged slowly from the aethers, faint as a sliver of Moon. Lilit circled round her, barely recognising her form.

"You look like a wraith, Lilith," I said, unable to hide my distress. "Is it Sol Niger that makes us frail and dim like this?"

"It is the time when Witches and Sorcerers have been cleaved from the Angels," she said.

"The Harmony is lost. Mortals no longer wish to see the Dark that walks with the Light. They fear what lies hidden in their shadows, forgetting that their greatest Wisdom abides therein."

"But how will they ever restore the Harmony of the Light and Dark within them?"

"You saw this progression as well as I, Hekate," she said. "The mortals must first learn to face the Dark, to face their Truth again. To do so, they must endure their own black descent, their nigredo. It is their powerful resistance to their shadows you feel. We must endure the suffering along with them."

As she spoke, I felt an enormous wave of grief engulf me as if my whole existence were being crushed. I knew that Lilith was experiencing her own death throes, an Eye of the Fire as I had. Yet she saw it as the inevitable precursor to Regeneration and Transformation—the Dark that needed to be borne.

"Time and time again, it is left to femina to Regenerate and Transform, to lead the way," I said, my voice loud in my ears. "How can we do so when we have been abandoned?"

My suffering turned to rage at all the injustices I had witnessed. It surged within me like a giant oak being set ablaze.

"I have carried the pain of the abandoned Great Mother for far too long," I cried out. "You have too, Lilith. I know you have!"

"Always remember Hekate, there is no power greater than the Great Mother," she said. "She is forever etched in mortal's Heart-Souls."

"You and I may be the last vestiges of her living Truth," she added, "but I am the Crone, the one of all Knowing, who waits to reawaken her Ancient power and bring mortal hubris to its knees."

I wept as she spoke, feeling both her suffering and her immense strength. Tears of Compassion coursing through me, cleansing the rage and pain at my core. Yet the grief remained. She began to fade and disappear like rain at twilight.

"We must stay the course and be present where we can. This, too, shall pass."

"No, Lilith, do not go yet!" I pleaded.

"Stay the course," she said in a whisper as she vanished. "The Great Change shall come. And we shall return in full force when the time is right."

We mourned together, The Many and I, at how profoundly we had waned. The Elementals and Sprites of Nature, who had been alongside the mortals in the fields and forests, streams and oceans, all waned along with us. The mortals looked around them with fearful faces before opening to the Realms to honour Earth's spirits. They had abandoned the old rituals and celebrations of the Moon, burying their amulets in haystacks or hiding them in tree trunks. Some dropped their treasures down deep wells, lest they be found out and tortured and burned as Witches.

Lilith and I had stopped being consulted by the mortals. It was as if the door between us had been bolted shut. My only consolation was that the ones called Wisewomen and Wisemen kept the Ancient herb-lore and healing remembered, albeit hidden from sight. Their knowledge was feared by the conquerors. The Wise ones that practiced the art were seized and forced to reveal their secrets so the conquerors could become masters of it themselves.

I had brought the Knowing with me from antiquity, from the times when we intuited what was needed for healing. My Goddess-daughters Medusa and Circe, and her daughter Medea, had continued the legacy. But they, too, were punished or banished for the power of their innate gifts.

We knew we would have to wait until a new wave of mortals rose from the aethers of existence to reclaim the Knowing and recreate the Alchemy of Healing for them all. It was a painfully long gestation, a time of great trials asking great patience from Lilith and me. We remained true to our undying faith in the Wisdom of the Eternal Round and the Infinite Light. We watched and we waited. But always, we *knew*. We would return.

PART FIVE

The Infinite Light of Eternity

"There is a Moon inside every human being.
Learn to be companions with it.
Give more of your life to this listening."
– Rumi

Lilith's Homecoming

As each new era dawned, Lilith and I watched, ever hopeful, as fragments of Knowing floated in the aethers, stirring traces of memory, echoes of things faintly remembered. Slowly, the Knowing wound its way into mortals' dreams like tales on papyrus torn from the Ancient scrolls. In time, mortals began seeking tales from the days of Isis and the Hellenes. They began hearing whispers from the Celtic Realm as the dwindling forests and streams sang songs of remembrance.

"Images of the Goddess still speak to the mortals," I said to Lilith. "The quiet voice of Mother Mary has prevailed. Mary Magdalene now embodies the forgotten Divine. Dear Brigid has become a saint. Kuan Yin remains the guide of Compassion in the Far East. Kali and Shakti are but two of many Goddesses beloved in the silk and spice lands."

"It is as I foretold," Lilith said. "The Knowing of Divine Femina could never be silenced and lost forever."

But in truth Divine Femina, who led mortals with the sway of the one-gods, had ceased to exist. It was only Witches who honoured Nature's holiness and the Great Mother, the triple Goddess in her forms as Maid, Mother, and Crone. And they were as maligned and feared as they had been in the past.

I watched as Margaret Murray, whom mortals later called Grandmother of Wicca, felt the awakening of the Ancient Knowing ride within her. I gently guided the pull she felt to visit the land of Isis in Egypt, sensing that the Goddess heritage and the mysteries of Witchery lay buried there. I knew her fearless intuiting would awaken even more as she travelled to the Sacred, honey-sweet isle they now called Malta. There Goddess stories spoke from every stone, vestiges of Priestess times scattered far and wide on rocky outcrops and buried deep in caves for her to see. Although she wrote what she had learned about Witchery in her books, it was only fragments of Knowing she was able to see, and others fought to discredit even those findings.

Like Margaret, Gerald Gardner, too, had felt the pull of the Ancient Knowing of Witchery. Since Witchery had been given a bad name, I whispered the word Wicca to him, the old word for sorcery, along with his witchcraft name, Scire. He wrote of his Knowings, drawing on the writing of others who had felt the tug of the Ancients in their Being.

Doreen Valiente was another mortal who had heard Lilith and me through the aethers. As Wiccan Priestess, she brought our stories of the Dark Goddess and Divine Femina to Light, along with a deep understanding of Earth's mysteries. She became the Mother of modern Witchery, not allowing her written words to be corrupted by male-kind.

The Wiccans honoured the blessings of the Earth, just as my kin in the Celtic Realm had done. Little by little, they grew in number, following their inner Knowings and the codes and rituals of the Realms. And little by little, like long forgotten music buried deep in memory, Lilith and I were resurrected, sung back into existence.

"I have spoken with the Goddesses in the pantheon and my kin in the Celtic Realm," I told Lilith. "They, too, have seen the shift in Earth's orbit. They, too, have heard the mortals' plea for a better world."

"The waiting is over, Hekate," she said, her tone resolute. "The portals are opening. At last, we are here again, Divine Femina renewed."

"We may be visible now, but the Knowing of us is only in its infancy," I said.

"We are visible because the time for the Great Transformation has come," she said. "The myths of conquerors and powermongers no longer fool the mortals. Earth is being despoiled of Nature's gifts. Mortals no longer feast around fires with their kin. They are lost in a world of endless cravings, with no understanding of Spirit to guide them. We will give them strength and renewed Wisdom. And solace for their dread of the shadow within them."

"Will there be enough mortals who can see and hear us, enough to make a difference?" I asked.

"They have found silence in their prayers. They will hear us. And in the stillness, they will come to see us."

She drew herself into her full, emblazoned and terrifying form, uttering a roar so penetrating it untethered the Moon's magnetic pull and rocked the Earth from side to side like a child's toy boat. Tidal waves rose from the oceans, obliterating the lands from the widest plain to the tallest mountain. Mortals engulfed in the flood looked like tiny figures with their arms aloft. It was a horrifying conjuration she had shown me. And I suspect it was a measure of her rage at their abandonment of us.

"Is that what awaits them, awaits Earth?" I whispered.

"Not if I have anything to do with it," she said. "But the golden mirrors of distraction will need to be put aside. The mortals must pay attention before it is too late."

I should have known that Lilith, as always, had already divined a path.

"We must enter their yearning through their dreams and symbols. We must part the walls they have built within themselves and enter their innermost Being through the depths of the Moon," she said. "And we must call on every god of their faiths, even the gods of greed and vanity. It is time."

She had returned to her former glory with a radiance more powerful than in any other existence I had witnessed. As she rose to her complete fullness, I shrank away from her, fearing another devastating conjuration.

"Those of vision that speak with Compassion and Love are calling to those who are lost," she said. "All mortals must be fully awake for such tasks. They have been hypnotized into a walking sleep. But while the greed for riches prevails, it is Gaia herself that is awaking them from their slumber. Their deserts grow wider, and food becomes scarce. Their waters are awash with waste and poison ..."

"Please, Lilith, stop!" I wailed. "I already know of this. And they know as well."

"The ones who wield the power must be named aloud," said Lilith. "Many of them are hidden. They must be flushed out and held to account at every turn."

"The mortals are speaking up and naming the offenders, Lilith," I argued. "But the reach of the power-mongers is too great. They diminish the resistors by shaming, by force, by murder. They eliminate and destroy them. They do not want to share their wealth. They cannot bear to face their own demise. They will never relinquish their power."

Lilith stayed silent for a moment.

"It is simple, but it is not easy. I have returned because the mortals seek answers. They speak of change all over the orb. They can spread the word and heal themselves and the Earth faster than the ills that plague them. This is their power. Find the speakers of Heart-Soul, the scribes and the artists among them, the poets and healers, the music-makers, the Witches and the Shamans. Find whomever and whatever it takes to bring Heart-Soul back to life. Find every form of existence that enkindles them and breathes Light back into their Being."

"But they have forgotten the Knowing of Heart-Soul, and the Knowing that the elders, the Crone, and the Senex bring," I said. "How will that change?"

"It is true that change will be hard won," Lilith continued. "But Seers and Knowers are awakening in numbers far greater than ever before. They do not yet know it is the fearless Wisdom of the Crone they hear. It is her voice that has been silenced too long in the Cosmos."

Her stature grew and grew as she spoke, until her presence was as powerful and omnipotent as in her prime. She was a sight to behold, filling the Cosmos with the dark void and luminous pearl of her Great Spirit, the greatest Crone of All.

"We are their helpers, Hekate. We are links in the Chain of Being. We are the Light in the Dark Moon to banish the old ties. Let the Death of the old and the cleansing of Transformation truly begin. Let us behold the upsurge of the strength and numbers of mortals who rise to the call. They are opening to the Infinite Light, awakening the Divine Femina and Dark Crone within them. They will bring Divine Wisdom back to Earth's portal from the Sleep of Ages. It is time. The Mysteries of the Cosmos are theirs for the asking."

Moon Dance

As Lilith and I communed, a bright halo encircled the Full Moon as it poised on the rim of Earth's horizon. We could see many awakened mortals illuminated in its light, as if the crystalline eyes of the Atlanteans had reemerged through the Cosmos.

"The era of Pure Radiance on Earth has begun," Lilith said. "It is your covenant with the Cosmos to guide mortals in a rhythmic dance with the Moon, Hekate. You are the oracular Light of the Dark Moon. Now is the time to show them they are all Beings of Light."

I placed my hands in the sign of the dove, praying deeply as I reached out to the orbs and powers of the Cosmos.

"Ancients from all the realms and beyond, I call on you to send your Wisdom to the mortals' Knowing, held in the silent space between their every breath."

As the Ancients drew near, the Light of the Cosmos shone through the grids of Earth again, refracting into a rainbow of pulsating colour. Mortals and Beings alike were bathed in its light, a jewelled web of vibrating colour.

"Teach us," I heard mortals say. "Tell us of the Mysteries and Wisdom of the Ancient Ones."

Lilith nodded to me to respond. It was hard to grasp that we had finally returned after aeons of invisibility. I could feel the power of the Cosmos aligning within me as I became visible to the mortals. I prepared myself to speak.

"The Divine Femina has returned to dance with the rhythms of the Moon," I began. "Just as the Moon guides the ebb and flow of the oceans, so too does the Divine weave through the watery blood of your veins. Let your senses awaken with each of her phases, each subtle change of the Femina Moon. Be in tune with all of Nature. Let the rhythm of your breath and the flow of your blood pulse in unity with the Divine, all dancing together as one. Honour the merging of your heartfelt Intention with the Divine spark within you, so that you may Know your true purpose on Earth."

"Keep going," Lilith said to me, glowing like a luminous black pearl. "Speak first of The Birthing Moon."

My voice could be heard as an Oracle of Light as it emerged from the Darkness of the umbra at the very heart of the Moon. The words came to me as pure and clear as the music of the spheres.

"When the Birthing Moon dawns as a thread of Light, you must go within to find the spark of fire to begin your new life. Your hopes and aspirations will first awaken in you as urges and dreams. Listen to what you long for in your Heart-Soul. Give wings to your vision. It is the seed of your own Tree of Life."

I could hear mortals speaking back to me, some in my own Ancient tongue, enlivened, wanting to know more.

"Next comes the Budding Moon. As her crescent expands, the seed you have planted will appear in the Light as a tiny green bud to nurture. Doubts and hesitations may come. Fears of unworthiness, of failure, of heartache. Sometimes they will come as wounds, hurting and stabbing at you, driving you away from the Light. Remember, they are only thoughts, nothing more. Treat them with kindness and Compassion, like those who need your Love and faith in them. Heal your wounds with the calming of your breath."

The Ancient Ones came forth to urge me on with my discourse. They stood beside me like towering obelisks against the starry Cosmos. The surge of Light from their presence flooded the Earth, magnifying the glow of the grids.

"As she reaches her first quarter, she becomes the Refining Moon. Your bud has grown leaves, and the roots have reached deeply into the cool Earth. Conflicts may erupt from within and without, threatening to uproot you. Hold fast to the vision you saw in the darkness. Hold fast to Compassion. Be true to your own path, the path to the deep Knowing of yourself. Keep breathing calmness into your Being."

Inanna came forth to stand alongside me. The others gathered round me in the half-circle of a crescent Moon. I heard their chorus of voices chanting my words all over the Cosmos.

"When the Moon's Light grows to gibbous, it has become the Auspicious Moon. The fruit on your Tree begins to ripen, and you must hold fast through the challenges of wind and rain, heat and cold, knowing fullness is nearing. You are learning to stay the course."

The Light of Transformation streamed through the Dark Moon within me, and I knew to speak on without hesitation.

"As the fullness of the Divine Femina Moon is reached, all is revealed. This is the Harvest Moon, the fertile peak in the cycle. Your seed of hope may now have ripened into fruit filled with new seeds. Or it may have failed and fallen back to the Earth's embrace to await another time, and you will reseed your intention. If you have found abundance with your Tree, celebrate success, but do not boast of it."

"At Harvest Moon time, Earth is poised like a pendulum between the Sun and the Moon. Be watchful of fears and troubles that may arise within and unbalance you. If you swing out of Harmony, let go of wounds and heartaches through your tears and soothing breath. Take nothing to heart. Disappointments, shocks, and aches arise only to teach us inner strength. Clear sight and Compassion will restore you. Stay the course."

All the learning I had gained and the inroads I had made in my Transformation reached their peak as I spoke the Wisdom. As I sent gratitude and Love to my beloved kin in the Celtic realm and the realms beyond, I knew what to say next.

"The waning Gratitude Moon is the time when your tree has borne its fruit and the seeds are scattered from its withering form. The Ancestors, the Crone, and the Senex have brought you their teaching. It is time for you to share the gnosis, your deepening Wisdom, and offer thanksgiving for what you have received."

Many of the mortals were nodding, feeling a resonance within them for the Wisdom they had forgotten but always known. To strengthen their Knowing, Lilith opened the galaxy gates. She invoked the full force of the Cosmos to raise the Earth to its highest vibration. The Alchemy of her own Great Transformation had expanded her Light beyond my power to comprehend it. The chorus of Beings around me had multiplied a thousandfold, and now there were many from galactic portals beyond my Knowing. The magnitude of it all made me falter.

"Continue, Hekate," she said. "You are a conduit for us all. Your words are bringing mortals the keys to the Cosmos."

I did as she requested, feeling the Sacred Harmony spread through me in waves of rhythmic perfection.

"At the last crescent Forgiveness Moon, order must be maintained. It is time for the Tree to discard its unneeded leaves. It is a time of Transition, of baring yourself like the empty limbs of the Tree. There may be joys within you, and there may be lamenting. Allow space for your lingering tears, hurts, loss, and sadness. This is the time of meaning-making. The Paradox of Knowing that joy walks hand in hand with sorrow will emerge in you. Practise the art of holding both as one and see the Promise of Joy in every heartache. Let go of what could have been. Let go of the beauty that has faded and gone. The practice of breathing Forgiveness into the very bones of your Being will smooth the path of healing."

Looking down on the Earth from the Light of the Moon I could see that many mortals had placed their hands on their Heart-Soul in the sign of the Eternal Goddess. That was how the robes had taught them to pray, to ask for Forgiveness. But it was the Ancient symbol for Truth and Unity they had resurrected, the remembrance of the Light within them. The Divine Femina was coming back to life.

"And finally, the Dark Moon of Surrender," I said. "As she darkens to invisibility, it is time to detach and go within. Having scattered the seeds of renewal, the Tree now rests. The cycle is complete. The Dark Moon time is for cleansing and healing, the Transformation of clearing away the old to regenerate new growth. The Forgiveness Moon has prepared you for this most important of your tasks, the final letting go. Trust that the Ancients and ancestors walk with you. They live in the marrow of your bones. Trust in the Angel of Knowing that guides you. Its source is the Light within you, the song of Love and Wisdom that lies in your Heart."

I turned to the chorus of ethereal Beings around me, spreading my arms wide to the Infinite Light in the Ancient gesture of Gratitude. Turning back to the mortals, I could see the vivid Light of the Heart-Soul ablaze within them. Together, from the farthest reaches of the Cosmos to the very core of the indigo Earth, we had ushered in a new aeon.

"I, Hekate, will always be here in the Sacred Silence of the Light in the Dark Moon with my keys and my torches to guide the way for you. It is the place where your name is inscribed, the place where the seed of your Eternal Soul lies waiting to be renewed. There is nothing to fear. It is your home. Blessed Be."

READER'S GUIDE
BOOK CLUB DISCUSSION

1. *Behold* begins with a quote from the famous analytical psychologist Carl Jung, "There is no coming to consciousness without pain. People will do anything, no matter how absurd, in order to avoid facing their own Soul. One does not become enlightened by imagining figures of light, but by making the darkness conscious." What did Jung mean by this statement? Where do you see these themes playing out in the novel? Do you recognise this quest in your own life?

2. The story goes on to introduce a wide cast of characters from myth and folklore. Are there any characters you are already familiar with? Were there any surprises in the author's portrayal of these characters? Which characters were completely new to you? Did any stand out as a mythological figure you want to learn more about, or perhaps reflected an aspect of yourself?

3. The tension between Western religion and the goddess tradition is a central theme in the book. What are the major differences between these beliefs? Did *Behold* inform -and perhaps transform - your understanding of spirituality and inner knowing?

4. The archetype of the Crone, the Elder Wise-Woman has been resurrected and revered in *Behold*. The elder

woman has been marginalised in our society. Do you see evidence of aging and aged women re-emerging as a source of Wisdom and strength?

5. Why do you think the author chose Hekate as the narrator of *Behold*? How did this enhance the story? How does Hekate's storytelling give insights about her mentor Lilith?

6. Power, control, abuse and cruelty figure prominently in the novel from the portrayal of Zeus and the Olympeians to the "black robes" rising to power. Are there parallels in our contemporary world? Can you find examples of leadership that show the emergence of a new Femina paradigm?

7. With the decline and negation of the Sacred Femina, Hekate experiences profound grief, loss and depression entering a state which she calls "the Nigredo," (p.95) an alchemical term meaning decomposition. How do Hekate's visions help her get through these "long, lonely black descents" (p.95)? Why is it necessary for Hekate to undergo this ordeal?

8. Hekate and Lilith refer to Birth, Death and Rebirth as the "Eternal Round" (p.179), as cyclical and eternal rather than linear and finite. Persephone also refers to Death as the "Great Mystery" (p.89) What if we reframed our perception of life and death in this way? How would that change us? Do you think as a society we have a collective dread and fear of death?

9. Awakening and Transformation are also key themes in *Behold*. In what ways does the protagonist awaken and transform as her journey unfolds? How does her mentor Lilith guide and support her through this process? Does Lilith herself undergo a transformation?

10. Consider the significance of Hekate's relationship with Carnonos in the Celtic Realm? What does she learn from this union? How does their love match compare to that of Brigid and Bres the Beautiful?

11. *Behold* depicts the time period of "witch hunts" differently than mainstream textbooks. Were there any aspects you found interesting or disturbing? Were you aware of the Malleus Maleficarum before reading this novel? Why do you think the negative connotation of the word Witch has persisted? How might life on Earth be different if Nature worship, paganism and witchery were valued forms of faith and healing like traditional religions?

12. The final chapter Moondance gives the reader a meditative and reflective practice and offers hope for the future of Earth and all sentient beings. Do you pay attention to the changing phases and cycles of the Moon? Where do you see its influence? How can you bring more Moon Wisdom into your life?

13. Imagine a Femina deity with the primacy of the patriarchal God of traditional religions. What if Mother, Daughter and Holy Spirit were to prevail alongside the Holy Trinity (Father, Son and Holy Ghost)? How would that change the way of things in the world?

GLOSSARY

Greek Mythos
Although the descriptions of the various Goddesses and Gods are in keeping with generally accepted mythological readings, I have taken some poetic licence in the interpretation of the roles to shift the patriarchal bias.

<u>**The Titanides and Titans**</u>: the first order of Goddesses and Gods created by Gaia (Earth) and Ouranus (the heavens)

Atlas: A younger Titan, God of Endurance

Epimetheus: A younger Titan, God of Afterthought. Brother to Prometheus and husband of Pandora (see below)

Euronyme: A younger Titanide, Goddess of Water-Meadows and Pastures

Helios: A younger Titan who became the Sun God

Hekatoncheires: Fifty-headed, hundred-handed monsters, including Cottus the furious, Gyges the long-limbed, and Aegaeon the sea goat

Kronos: God of the Heavens. Father of the six major Goddesses and Gods of the Olympieions

Leto: A younger Titanide, Goddess of Light and Invisibility, impregnated by Zeus while everyone around her was distracted from protecting her by Ekho's echoes. Mother of Artemis and Apollo

Metis: A younger Titanide, Goddess of Wise Intuition. Mother of Athena

Prometheus: A younger Titan, God of Forethought

Themis: The Oracle. Goddess of Divine Law and Earth's Natural Order

Rhea: Goddess of Earth's Fertility. Mother of the six major Goddesses and Gods of the Olympieions

Other Titanides (Rhea's sisters) include: Mnemosyne (Memory and Language), Phoebe (Intellect), Tethys (Waters and Oceans), Theia (Light of the Ether)

The Olympieions: The second order of Goddesses and Gods, and the inhabitants of Mount Olympos. Also referred to as the pantheon of the Hellenes

The offspring of Rhea and Kronos:

Demeter: Goddess of the Harvest and the Fertility of the Earth. Keeper of the Eleusinian Rites, the secret ancient rituals of visioning the afterlife to transform the fear of death. Persephone's mother

Hades: God of the Underworld

Hera: Goddess of Union, Childbirth and Family. Mother of Ares and Hephaistos. Ruled with Zeus

Hestia: Goddess of the Sacred Altar, Hearth and Home

Poseidon: God of the Oceans

Zeus: God of Olympos

Their offspring:

Ares: God of Warring. Son of Hera and Zeus

Artemis: Goddess of the Hunt and Wild Nature. She was also Goddess of Chastity. Her mother was the Titanide Leto, and her twin was the god Apollo. Zeus was their father

Athena: Goddess of Courage, Warfare, Law, Civilisation, Arts and Handcrafts. Daughter of the Titanide Metis, and Zeus. In later accounts, she was said to have arisen from Zeus's head

Dionysus: God of Wine, Theater and Intoxication. His father was Zeus, and his mother Semele, a mortal

Hephaistos: God of Metallurgy and Blacksmiths. Son of Hera, rejected by Zeus because of his limp. He created a daughter, Pandora

Hermes: Messenger of the Gods and Divine Trickster. His mother was Maia, one of the Pleiades, and his father was Zeus

Persephone: Goddess of Spring and Queen of the Underworld. Assisted her mother Demeter with the Eleusinian Mystery Rites

Additional characters:

Aphrodite: Ancient Goddess of Love and War

Alcmene: A mortal princess who was impregnated by Zeus disguised as Alcmene's lover and bore Heracles, a Divine Hero in the pantheon

Baubo: Ancient Goddess of Mirth Wisdom

Ekho: An Oread (mountain nymph) who unwittingly supported Zeus's seduction of Leto through her capacity to repeat what had just been said, creating the illusion of listening intently to every word

Gorgons: Three sisters (Stheno, Euryale and Medusa) who moved between the Underworld and the Outer World, terrifying with their presence

Maia: The oldest of the sisters of the constellation of Pleiades, impregnated by Zeus and mother of Hermes

Melissa: The honeybee Goddess whose daughters and nymphs were known as the Melissaea

Pandora: Created by Hephaistos at Zeus's request to become the wife of Epithemeus as part of a plot to punish Prometheus

Semele: Daughter of Harmonia and Cadmus, a mortal princess of Thebes, who was impregnated by Zeus. Mother of Dionysus

Underworld characters:

Cerberus: Three-headed Watchdog of the Underworld

Charon: Ferryman of the Underworld rivers that divide the world of the living from the dead

Chimera: A fire-breathing hybrid creature

Erinyes: Also known as the Furies. The three Goddesses of retribution

Harpies: Monsters with the form of a bird with a female face who abducted, tortured, and punished people on the way to the Underworld

Hydra: A serpentine, many-headed water monster of the Underworld

Thanatos: Guardian at the Doors of the Underworld

Otherworld mythos:

Daimons: Semidivine spirits that either reflect shadow or light. In shadow form they become fearsome, denied aspects who grow to be distorted

Nigredo: The putrification process of the four stages of alchemy. The others are albedo (purification), citrinatis (transmutation), rubedo (transformation)

Ouroborous: Ancient symbol of unity depicted by the image of a serpent/dragon eating its own tail

Lemniscate: A symbol of Infinity

The Celtic Realm

Abnoba of Gaul: Goddess of the Hunt

Anu, Morrigan, Badb: triple Goddess, Maiden, Mother and Crone, Goddess of Birth, Life and Death

Bres: Leader of the Formoire

Brigid: Goddess of Spring, Fertility, Wisdom Keeper of the Sacred Flame, Queen of the Realm

Carnonos: Horned God of Nature. Also known as the Green Man

Cyrridwen: Goddess of Grain, Magic and Transformation

Devic Kingdom of Nature Spirits and Elementals

Draiochta (pl) / Draiocht (s): Druids of Antiquity

Eriu: the eponymous Goddess of Eire, Goddess of the Land

Formoire (pl) / Formoir (s): Enormous supernatural beings from the Underworld and Oceans

Medbh: Goddess of Battle and Sacred Marriage. Protector of the Sacred Groves of the Draiochta

Myrddin: Elder of the Draiochta, Magician and Shaman

Morrigan: see Anu (above)

Rhiannon: Moon Goddess, Queen of the Faeries

The Dagda: All-Father of the Tuatha de Danaan

Tuatha De Danaan (pl)/ Tuath de (s): Supernatural beings from the Otherworld who co-existed with humans

Deamhan: Demons of Celtic folklore, usually malevolent and troublesome

Succubi: Demons with female forms who seduce men in their sleep. Related to religious corruption

Lilit: Ancient supernatural owl gifted to Hekate (by Athena)

Diona and Nonos: Supernatural dogs gifted to Hekate (by Artemis)

Senex: in Jungian psychology the Senex is the archetype of the elder male wisdom figure.

READING LIST

Almaas, A.H. *The Pearl Beyond Price.* Berkeley, California: Diamond Books, 1988.

Bolen, Jean Shinoda. *Goddesses in EveryWoman.* New York: Harper Collins, 1984.

Campbell, Joseph. *The Power of Myth.* New York: Bantam Doubleday, 1991.

Christ, Carol P. *She Who Changes. Reimagining the Divine in the World.* New York: Palgrave MacMillan, 2003.

Corbett, Lionel. *The Religious Function of the Psyche.* New York: Brunner Routledge, 1996.

Edinger, Edward F. *The Mystery of the Coniunctio.* Toronto: Inner City Books, 1994.

Estes, Clarissa Pinkola. *Women Who Run with the Wolves.* London: Random House, 1992.

Fry, Stephen. *Mythos: A Retelling of the Myths of Ancient Greece.* London: Penguin Books, 2017.

George, Demetra. *Mysteries of the Dark Moon.* New York: HarperCollins Publishers, 1992.

Graves, Robert. *The Greek Myths.* New York: Penguin Books, 2012.

Graves, Robert. *The White Goddess.* (4th ed.). New York: Farrar, Straus & Giroux, 2013.

Helminski, K. *The Knowing Heart.* Boston: Shambhala, 1999.

Houston, Jean. *The Hero and the Goddess*. New York: The Aquarian Press, 1993.

Hillman, James. *Revisioning Psychology*. New York: Harper Row, 1975.

Hyde, Lewis. *Trickster Makes This World*. New York: Farrar, Straus & Giroux, 1998.

Jung, C.J. *Modern Man in Search of a Soul*. New York: Harcourt, Brace & World, 1933.

Keleman, Stanley. *Myth and the Body*. Berkeley, California: Center Press, 1999.

Le Grice, Keiron. *The Archetypal Cosmos*. Edinburgh: Floris Books, 2010.

McGilchrist, Iain. *The Master and his Emissary*. London: Yale University Press, 2009.

Neumann, Erich. *The Great Mother*. (7th ed.). Princeton: Princeton University Press, 1991.

Perera, Sylvia Brinton. *Descent to the Goddess*. Toronto: Inner City Books, 1981.

Sleeman, Lauren Ann. *The Forgotten Feminine: A Hermeneutic Phenomenological Study of Psychotherapists/Counsellors Who Work With Unusual Phenomena*. Master of Health Science thesis. Auckland, New Zealand: Auckland University of Technology, 2007.

Sleeman, Lauren. *La Magdalena. The Story of Mary*. Xlibris, 2013.

Stanton, Marlan. *The Black Sun*. USA: Texas A&M University Press, 2005.

Von Franz, Marie-Louise. *Redemption Motifs in Fairy Tales*. Toronto: Inner City Books, 1980.

Von Franz, Marie-Louise. *Shadow and Evil in Fairy Tales.* Boston: Shambhala, 1995.

Walker, Barbara G. *The Crone: Woman of Age, Wisdom and Power.* New York: Harper & Row, 1985.

Walker, Barbara G. *The Women's Encyclopedia of Myths and Secrets.* London: HarperCollins Publishers, 1983.

CPSIA information can be obtained
at www.ICGtesting.com
Printed in the USA
LVHW030107090821
694770LV00004B/448